A MARXIST READING OF FUENTES, VARGAS LLOSA AND PUIG

Dr. Victor Manuel Durán

Millikin University
Decatur, Illinois

UNIVERSITY
PRESS OF
AMERICA

Lanham • New York • London

Copyright © 1994 by
University Press of America®, Inc.
4720 Boston Way
Lanham, Maryland 20706

3 Henrietta Street
London WC2E 8LU England

Library of Congress Cataloging-in-Publication Data

Durán, Víctor M. (Víctor Manuel)
A Marxist reading of Fuentes, Vargas Llosa, and Puig /
Víctor Manuel Durán.
p.   cm.
Includes bibliographical references and index.
1. Spanish American fiction—20th century—History and criticism.
2. Fuentes, Carlos. Muerte de Artemio Cruz.   3. Vargas Llosa,
Mario, 1936–   Casa verde.   4. Puig, Manuel. Boquitas pintadas.
5. Communism and literature.   I. Title.
PQ7082.N7D87   1993   863—dc20   93–27214 CIP

ISBN 0–8191–9305–4 (cloth : alk. paper)

 The paper used in this publication meets the minimum requirements of
American National Standard for Information Sciences—Permanence
of Paper for Printed Library Materials, ANSI Z39.48–1984.

For Adela, Arelí Amira, Myrna Leticia, Nadia Karina and Shanta Celeny-you have helped me more than you will ever know-thanks!

For my mother and all my brothers and sisters and for all my friends in Progreso, where it all started...

CONTENTS

PREFACE

There is no doubt that the contemporary literature from Latin America is now at the forefront of world literature. Internationally recognized Spanish-American writers like José Donoso, Carlos Fuentes, Mario Vargas Llosa, the late Manuel Puig, and Isabel Allende, to name a few, have revitalized and popularized Spanish-American letters through their varied and distinctive narrative techniques, their "invented" vocabulary and their precise combination of myth and reality. Each of these writers, in their respective texts, explore and define the polifaceted characteristics of the culture of Latin America and address the complex issue of the Latin American's search for identity. It is almost impossible to have an understanding of Latin-American culture without reading the novels of the above-mentioned writers, particularly those of Fuentes, Vargas Llosa and Puig.

As a Latin-American from Central America I was imbued, from birth, with traditional cultural values which surround every Latin American, whether he be raised in Latin America or elsewhere. I was fascinated and intrigued by the criticism of these values that the literature of Latin-America makes, particularly as reflected in the contemporary novels. My interest grew as I delved more and more into Spanish-American letters and was fostered and encouraged by some of my professors as I struggled to complete my graduate studies; the result is this text, which I hope will illuminate the contents of three selected Latin-American novels.

ACKNOWLEDGEMENTS

I would like to thank Dr. Daniel Scroggins, Associate Professor of Latin-American Literature at the University of Missouri-Columbia for his invaluable suggestions, corrections, recommendations and textual revisions when this project was in its embryonic and most important stage.

I would also like to thank Helen Nelson from Millikin University for generously donating her time and technical knowledge in helping me prepare this manuscript.

INTRODUCTION

There have been a number of critical studies that have been written on Carlos Fuentes's *La Muerte de Artemio Cruz (1962)*, Mario Vargas Llosa's *La Casa Verde* (1966) and Manuel Puig's *Boquitas Pintadas* (197O). Among these many studies are the following: on *La Muerte de Artemio Cruz: Social Reform in Selected Works of Carlos Fuentes* by Judy Kay Ferguson-Salinas;[1] *Carlos Fuentes:Literatura y Sociedad* by Luis Manuel Villar;[2] "Valores temáticos y estructurales en *La Muerte de Artemio Cruz*" by Ileana Araujo[3] and "La distorsión temporal y las técnicas cinematográficas en *La Muerte de Artemio Cruz*" by Linda S. Glaze.[4]

Vargas Llosa's *La Casa Verde* has prompted a great amount of critical articles and texts. Among these are the following: *Dependency Theory and Literary Analysis: Reflections on Vargas Llosa's The Green House* by M. J. Fenwick;[5] *Mario Vargas Llosa:La invención de una realidad* by José Miguel Oviedo;[6] "The web of defeat: a thematic view of characterization in Mario Vargas Llosa's *La Casa Verde*" by Michael Moody[7] and *From Lima to Leticia: The Peruvian novels of Mario Vargas Llosa* by Marvin Lewis.[8]

Manuel Puig's *Boquitas Pintadas* has not provoked as much literary criticism as have Fuentes's *Cruz* and Vargas Llosa's *La Casa Verde*. The following are some of the more important articles that have been published on *Boquitas: "El folletín rescatado"* by Emir Rodríguez Monegal;[9] Phyllis Mitchele's *"The Reel against the Real: Cinema in the novels of Guiellermo Cabrera Infante and Manuel Puig,"* [10] Jonathan Tittler's *"Order, chaos and re-order: The novels of Manuel Puig,"*[11] and Severo Sarduy's *"Notas a las notas...A propósito de Manuel Puig."*[12]

Although the critical works cited above are only samples of the many that have been published, they are indispensable for an understanding of the respective novels. With the exception of a few (for example Lewis's and Fenwick's texts) all of them analyze the novels from structural and narrative critical perspectives. It is my expectation that a Marxist reading of the three texts will provide a better comprehension of the sociopolitical content dealt with in each novel, as well as enhance the reader's knowledge of the nature of some of the problems faced by Latin-American writers. Marxist theory of literature gives precedence to interdependent characteristics of a society as they collectively function to make an environment what it is. This particular body of critical literary theory categorizes literature and art as only the manifested superstructures of a society, whose existence is dependent on the existence of an economic base. Since these three novels explore specific cultural and social aspects of three particular Latin-American countries, then it is suggested here that a Marxist reading of each will illuminate the content of each text.

This is not to say that a structuralist and purely linguistic critical approach may be inadequate for an understanding of these novels; on the contrary, elements of the language have to be studied and analyzed before a comprehensive historico-sociological interpretation can be validly rendered. The Latin-American novel of today is, in general, one of protest and criticism against an externally and/or internally imposed form of exploitation. Particular elements of the society, the politics, and the religion (that is, elements of the Marxist superstructure) are scrutinized through the use of a vibrant, popular and contemporary language. Since language is the only means a novelist has to express his ideas, then it is adapted, changed, subverted and sometimes vulgarized to reflect closely the emotions, ideas and, at times, psychosis of the characters that the writer realistically portrays.

In a critical reading of the modern Latin-American narrative it is impossible to separate the environmental factors which influenced the writer from the language he employed to write the novel. The language articulates the content and is adapted (sometimes with innovative adjustments in vocabulary and syntax) to mirror it. It is therefore evident that an analysis of the language is quite appropriate in discussing the Marxist literary concept that affirms that good literature portrays aspects of a historical reality. But the language can not be studied in isolation and can not be categorized as the only literary device that can classify the three novels as Marxist. Instead, it has to be perceived as one of the numerous literary recources that each of the authors inculcates in his particular work in order to help the reader better understand aspects of the social reality he depicts. If perceived in this manner, then language can be said to be part of the narrative structure that each author uses to reflect the content. It is in this light that language will be discussed in this analysis.

I chose Vargas Llosa's *La Casa Verde*, Fuentes's *La Muerte de Artemio Cruz* and Puig's *Boquitas Pintadas* for this analysis because in each of these novels the writers examine the impact of specific political, sociological and historical factors on a people and on a nation. Moreover, these three novels critically comment on Latin-American life in general and address and explore the complex issue of identity of the Latin-American individual.

Vargas Llosa, for example, combines in *La Casa Verde* factual historical events (the exploitation of Perú's rubber and cotton by foreign and national corporations) with fiction to demonstrate how a society changes under the influence of an exploitative and manipulative economic system. The novelist also explores the idea of entrapment as he describes the futile attempts of members of different social strata as they scheme to upgrade their social standing, without realizing that they are trapped in their particular economic niche and that they are the exploiters as well as the exploited. The actions and reactions of a people living under an imposed hierarchical society are some of the aspects of this novel that make it appropriate for a Marxist analysis.

Through an old and dying revolutionary, Fuentes, in *La Muerte de Artemio Cruz*, provides a critically panoramic view of present and past Mexican society. He explores the identity of the contemporary Mexican through the use of the "I," You" and "He" narrative structure. Through Artemio, Fuentes criticizes the underhanded methods employed by post-revolutionary Mexicans to acquire wealth. In the novel he also describes the negative effects that foreign monopoly capitalism has on the society as he details Cruz's preference for American made consumer goods. He inter-twines a verifiable historical event (the Mexican Revolution of 1910) with a representative fictional character (Artemio Cruz) to show how the lofty but achievable goals of the Revolution were betrayed.

Through Cruz, we also see the negative effects on a society that is divided between the haves and the have-nots. These particular characteristics of the novel create the conditions for a Marxist reading of it.

Puig, by means of the description of the inhabitants of Coronel

Vallejos in *Boquitas Pintadas*, levels criticism on the snobbish attitude of the "petit bourgeosie" of Argentina. He exposes the social divisions in Vallejos as artificial and self-imposed. He ridicules the hollowness and hypocrisy of the members of various social groups as he uncovers the dishonest methods they employ in their frantic attempt to "claw" their way to a higher social stratum. Puig also relegates the Argentine's consumption of foreign consumer goods (in this case foreign movies) to a form of foreign exploitation and domination. The class-divided society in Vallejos is in clear juxtaposition to the Marxist perception of a classless society and this is one of the many factors that preconditions this novel for a Marxist analysis.

I want to specify clearly here that it is not the intention of this text to classify any of these three novelists as Marxists. By the same token, I do not mean to imply or suggest that any of the novels I will analyze are Marxist. Rather, it is the purpose of this analysis to show that a *Marxist reading* of these three texts can help the reader better understand them since they contain Marxist elements of literary theory which, when explored, will render a better comprehension of the content of each novel and of the purpose of each respective novelist in writing it.

The present study analyzes elements of style, plot, structure and content of these three novels. The analysis uses salient characteristics of Marxist literary theory as expounded principally by Karl Marx (1818-1883), Frederick Engels (1820-1895) and their "disciples."

Chapter 1

Marxist Literary Theory

Any effort to present a coherent overview of Marxist literary theory is complicated by the fact that Marx's and Engels's philosophy of literature was not collected in a single text. Instead, it is scattered in many of their writings and the critic finds himself obliged to examine their works and glean from them their ideas on art and literature. This phenomenon occurs not because Marx and Engels were uninterested in literature. On the contrary, they were both avid readers of such popular writers as Balzac, Goethe, Dickens, and Shakespeare. The problem exists because it seems that they could not quite decide what the role of the artist should be in a classless, communist society. Indeed, after Marx's death, Engels re-explained some of their theories on art and literature in a series of letters which he sent to several writers of the period. It has to be noted that one of the major devices employed by both Marx and Engels to explain their theory on literature was analysis of texts they considered representative of their literary philosophy. Marxist literary theory in this analysis will be explained from interpretations made by well-known "apostles" of Marxist literary criticism, some of them being Terry Eagleton, Lee Baxandall, Stefan Morawski, Henri Arvon and Peter Demetz.

It is easier to comprehend Marxist philosophy, literary and otherwise, if one has some knowledge of some of Hegel's (1770-1831) philosophy. A brief outline of Hegel's concept of art and its influence on Marx is enough for the purpose of this study. The synthesis that follows is paraphrased from Henri Arvon's *Marxist Esthetics*.[1]

Hegel thought of the novel as the bourgeois representation of the epic. In his view, the novel originated from "the conflict between the poetry of the heart and the prose of the situation that is its opposite, losing itself in the exterior and the contingent" (quoted in Arvon, p.5). Hegel said that whereas in the epic the subjective is raised to the level of the typical, in the novel the relations between the subjective and the typical do not always correspond. Hegel takes Dutch painting of the seventeenth century as an example: He points out that Dutch painting reflects to a great degree the physical surroundings and the daily life of Dutchmen. About this he says:

> The joy the Dutch took in life, even in its most ordinary and trivial aspects [...] Stemmed from the fact that they were forced to conquer, at the price of a very difficult struggle and painful efforts, what nature offers other people without a struggle and without effort [...] The Dutch created most of the soil on which they live with their own hands; they were obliged to defend it ceaselessly against the assaults of the sea. This civic pride, this spirit of enterprise, this joyous and exuberant consciousness of self they owe entirely to their own efforts, to their own activity, and that is what constitutes the general content of their paintings (quoted in Arvon, pp. 5-6).

For Hegel there is a proportional relationship between the social forms and artistic forms of Dutch painting. Hegel's esthetic, through its analysis of details, demonstrates a process of evolution of human societies. Because it shows this process, Marx and Engels liked some of the writers of the bourgeois period (example Balzac and Fielding) since these writers commented on the social and political world in which they lived.

Marx however does not agree with the Hegelian thesis on the death and subsequent uselessness of art. Hegel believes there are three stages in the march of the spirit toward the Absolute. These stages are Art, Religion and Philosophy. Hegel says that art peaks in ancient Greece, that religion climaxes in Christianity and that philosophy raises both art and religion to the level of Absolute Knowledge. He asserts that when humanity achieves this stage of Absolute Knowledge then art becomes an outdated investigation of reality, a method that is now rendered as unimportant. For Hegel art is a temporary phase, a means to an end. Art for Hegel: "invites us to engage in a philosophical reflection whose aim is not to bring about its rebirth, but to acquire a rigorous knowledge of its essence" (quoted in Arvon, p.7). Hegel believes that for the modern epoch art is a thing of the past since its purpose has been served through the flourishing of ancient Greek art.

Although Marx also believes that art reached its pinnacle with the Greeks, he disagrees with Hegel's ideology on the origin and permanence of art. Marx perceives art as part of the overall evolution of humanity and believes in the existence of a dialectical relationship between art and the many political, social and economic stages through which mankind has evolved.

In his *Critique of Poltical Economy* Marx emphasizes a contradiction in our concept of Greek art which counters the Hegelian notion of the temporality of art. Marx examines and agrees with the specific historical factors which produced Greek art and led us to appreciate it; however, despite so many historical changes, Marx asks why is it that Greek art still holds a permanent attraction for humanity? He affirms that Greek art still offers us esthetic pleasure and in some senses, and for some modern artists, it serves as a peerless model. Looking at Greek art from this perspective, how can we accept Hegel's concept of the impermanence of art? Marx believes that we now appreciate Greek art because it expresses the magic of the infancy of humanity: it was only able to flourish in a very primitive phase of man's evolution. In his *Critique* Marx says:

> The attraction that their (Greek) art has for us, [...] is not in contradiction with the feeble development of the society in which it evolved. On the contrary, it is the result of it. It is indissolubly linked with the fact that the rudimentary state of society in which this art was born, the only one in which it could be born, wil never again recur (quoted in Arvon, p.8).

By linking Greek art to the society in which it was produced, Marx attempts to justify mankind's present esthetic appreciation of it. This concise paraphrase of Hegelian philosophy and its influence on Marxist esthetics leads us to the first dominant characteristic of Marx's literary theory. Karl Marx maintains that graphic arts and by extension literature, are part of a total human evolution and can not be isolated from it. He recognizes that art is part of the evolutionary process of a society and asserts this in his *Introduction to the Critique of Political Economy*:

> In the social production of their means of existence men enter into definite, necessary relations which are independent of their will, productive relationships which correspond to a definite stage of development of their material productive forces. The aggregate of these productive relationships constitutes the economic structure of society, the real basis on which a juridical and political superstructure arises, and to which definite forms of social consciousness correspond. The mode of production of the material means of existence conditions the whole process of social, political and intellectual life. It is not the consciousness of men that determines their existence, but on the contrary, it is their social existence that determines their consciousness.[2]

Marx says that the theoretical basis of literature is its relationship to society as a whole and that literature is a superstructure of social consciousness which has as its basis the productive relationship between different aspects of the society.

At first glance this dominant characteristic of Marxist literary theory suggests that literature and art will reflect only the level of total evolution of a given society and that they will not supersede this level; instead, the esthetic productivity of the society in question will proportionally reflect its entire evolutionary output. As is evident, this contradicted the esthetic production of ancient Greek civilization: at a time when their culture and economic productivity were very primitive, Greek art was flourishing. Marx was aware of this inherent contradiction in his theory and modified it in the same text quoted above:

> It is well known that certain periods of highest development of art stand in no direct connection with the general development of society, nor with the material basis and the skeleton structure of its organization. Witness the example of the Greeks compared with the modern nations and even Shakespeare (quoted in Hyman, p.545)

In this manner Marx explains that art, being part of the super-structure, is not totally determined by the behavior of the base, which to him is economic in nature. In an evolving society the relationship between the economic base and the artistic super-structure is not necessarily direct or proportional or even mechanically determined. Art can transcend not only the barriers of its very own social beginnings but also may supersede the artist's own point of view. This is why both Engels and Marx liked Balzac-he was able to supersede his own point of view in his novel *The Human Comedy.* Marx and Engels' admiration for Balzac is summed up in a letter which Engels wrote to Margaret Harkness in April of 1888. In it he says:

> ... Balzac was politically a Legitimist; his great work is a constant elegy on the irretrievable decay of good society; his sympathies are all with the class doomed to extinction. But for all that his satire is never keener, his irony never bitterer than when he sets in motion the very men and women with whom he sympathises most deeply-the nobles. And the only men of whom he speaks with undisguised admiration, are his bitterest political antagonists.... That Balzac thus was compelled to go against his own class sympathies and political prejudices, that he saw the necessity of the downfall of his favorite nobles, and described them as people deserving no better fate; and that he saw the real men of the future where, for the time being, they alone were to be found--that I consider one of the greatest triumphs of Realism, and one of the grandest features of Balzac.[3]

Engels further clarifies this contradiction between the dis-propotionate level of artistic and economic production in a society in a letter to Joseph Bloch, after the death of Marx. In it he states:

> According to the materialistic view of history, production and reproduction are ultimately the determining element in history in real life [...] But now if someone twists that around to mean that the economic element is the only determining one, then he transforms that proposition into a meaningless, abstract, absurd phrase. The economic situation is the basis, but the various elements of the superstructure-political forms of the class struggle and its results, constitutions established by the victorious class after the battle has been won, and so on-legal forms-and even the reflexes of all these real struggles in the minds of those taking part in them, political, legal, philosophical theories, religious ideas and their further development into systems of dogma-also have their effect upon the course of historical struggles and in many cases predominantly determine their form.[4]

For Marx and Engels there exists a mutual interdependency between the base and superstructure; however, as shown by the example of Greek art, esthetic sensibilities can supersede the economic base and flourish independently, regardless of the given level of evolution of any particular society.

A third dominant aspect of Marx's literary theory focuses on his analysis of the relationship between form and content in a work of art. Art, as part of the superstructure, has a dialectical relationship to other components of the superstructure and to the economic base. In literature, Marx contends that the content is a reflection of the evolutionary level of development of the society; this content is therefore expressed in a form which adequately represents it and which exhibits a unity between them, with the content being the determinant of the form. Because of this belief, Marx destroyed some of his earlier lyric poetry since he thought that the emotions portrayed in it were too unrestrained and exhibited an unbalanced relationship between form and content. For Marx, content had primacy over form, and he relegated the function of the latter to that of a vessel which embodies the revolutionary content. As Arvon clearly explains:

> Marxist esthetics, which considers the work of art to be intimately related to social life as a whole, is left no choice with regard to the relation between content and form. It is forced to admit the priority of content, which then creates the need for an appropriate form. Marxist esthetics is therefore necessarily an esthetics centered on content; and thus is situated at the opposite pole from all esthetics based on a gratuitous or arbitrary play of forms and also from any sort of formalism. The relations between content and form correspond to the more general relations between the economic base and the ideological superstructure; content is the governing factor, and though form in the final analysis is always necessarily subservient to it, it is not thereby shorn of all autonomy whatsoever (Arvon, p.41).

Marxist esthetics unequivocally gives primacy to content and associates the relationship between content and form to the relationship between base and superstructure.

It has to be realized that in postulating his theory on the relationship between form and content, Marx was, to some extent, adapting Hegel's philosophy on the same literary issue. In his *Philosophy of Fine Art* (1835), Hegel contends that "every definite content determines a form suitable to it," and he asserts that "Defectiveness of form...arises from defectiveness of content."[5] For Hegel, the ever changing relations between form and content is indeed the blueprint for writing the history of art. "Content," he (Hegel) wrote "is nothing but the transformation of form into content, and form is nothing but the transformation of content into form" (Eagleton, p. 22). For Marx form is the product of content and is determined by it. He thinks of form as being more stable and of content, since it reflects a historical evolution, as constantly changing. Form therefore lags behind content and in literature and art the former is then determined by the latter.

Marx shows a dialectical grasp of the relationship between form and content: while form is the product of content it can also react back upon it and make the content seem to appear to be determined by the form. Marx, in *Rheinische Zeitung* (a newspaper whih he edited in 1848-1849), said "form is of no value unless it is the form of its own content" (Eagleton, p. 21). Although this comment was made about law, it can also be applied to his esthetic views. Marx stresses his belief in the correspondence between form and content in a letter about the poetry of Chateaubriand which he sends to Engels in 1854. Part of this letter reads:

> In studying the Spanish cesspool, I fell upon the manipulations of the worthy Chateaubriand, that manufacturer of belles lettres who unites, in a most obnoxious manner, the polite scepticism and Voltairianism of the eighteenth century with the polite sentimentalism and romanticism of the nineteenth. This could not fail to be epoch-making in France from the point of view of style, although even in the style the falseness is often glaringly obvious, despite the artistic artifices.[6]

Marx not only derides Chateaubriand but also condemns the unorthodox application of form and content that he applied to his writing. He particularly denounces Chateaubriand's combination of sober scepticism with romantic sentimentality, which, in his mind, produces a dichotomy between form and content. Terry Eagleton provides a summary of Marx's philosophy on the correlation between form and content when he states:

> ... both thinkers (Marx and Hegel) share the belief that artistic form is no mere quirk on the part of the individual artist. Forms are

historically determined by the kind of "content" they have to embody; they are changed, transformed, broken down and revolutionized as that content itself changes. "Content" is in this sense prior to form, just as for Marxism it is changes in a society's material "content," its mode of production, which determine the "forms" of its superstructure (Eagleton, p. 113)

To this clear description of the Marxist concept of the relationship between form and content in literature, Fredric Jameson adds in *Marxism and Form* (1971): "Form itself is but the working out of content in the realm of the superstructure" (Eagleton, p. 22). Eagleton stipulates that although form and content are inseparable in practice, *Marxist criticism sees them as theoretically distinct* ("italicized" words are mine); he suggests that because of this conceptual distinction, Marx can assert the supremacy of content over form. In his *The Novel and the People* (1937), Ralph Fox emphasizes this distinction when he remarks: "Form is produced by content, is identical and one with it, and, though the primacy is on the the side of content, form reacts on content and never remains passive" (Eagleton, p.23).

As is now clear, Marx believed in a close correspondence between form and content, with content *dictating* form and *determining* its composition.

Another dominant trait of Marxist literary theory concerns the concept of reality in a work of art. Linked to this concept is the notion of "tendency" literature and in describing the Marxist concept of realism in literature one also has to describe Marx's concept of "tendency" writing. Marx insisted that literature does not have sophisticated esthetic techniques as its primary goal; rather, it is an essential component of a total social development. Art, for him, is a reflection of social reality and must inculcate its salient features. However, neither Marx nor Engels believed that literature is politically prescriptive. Marx's own favorite authors were Shakespeare and Goethe, neither of whom can be considered revolutionary. Rather, they were among his favorites because in their works they portrayed an aspect of social realism that reflected, to a great degree, the reality that they were experiencing.

Although Marx asserted that socialist realism is demonstrated in literature, he also insisted that the work of art by itself is not prescriptive. Political sympathies are part of Marx's criteria for evaluating literature; however, neither he nor Engels equated fine esthetic sensibilities with the politically correct. Marx liked realist and radical writers and detested Romanticism since he beleived that it cloaked the true realities of life. Marx and Engels's attitude towards realism is perhaps best summarized in a letter which Engels wrote to Minna Kautsky in 1885. She had sent him her novel *The Old and the New* (1884) for him to review and it was his reaction to this novel that illustrates his ideology on realism in the novel. He says :

> I am not at all an opponent of tendentious writing (*Tendenzpoesie*) as such [...] But I believe the tendency must spring forth from the situation and the action itself, without explicit attention called to it; the writer is not obliged to offer the reader the future historical solution of the social conflicts he depicts. Especially in our conditions [...] the socialist tendentious novel can fully achieve its purpose, in my view, if, by conscientiously describing the real mutual relations, it breaks down the conventionalized illusions dominating them, shatters the optimism of the bourgeois world, causes doubt about the eternal validity of the existing order, and this without directly offering a solution or even, under some circumstances, taking an ostensible partisan stand (Baxandall and Morawski, p. 113).

Engels agrees with fiction that shows a "political" tendency but suggests that it is wrong for a writer to be clearly partisan. He says that the political viewpoint emerges unobtrusively and in this manner is effective on the bourgeois consciousness of its readers. The novel is neither openly didactic nor does it offer a solution for the conflict it expresses.

In another letter (1888) to Margaret Harkness, Engels defines what he means by realism in literature. Miss Harkness had published a novel titled *City Girl* (1887) and had sent a copy to Engels to review. In his review he stipulated that the tale was not realistic enough since she portrayed the working class as passive, unable to help itself and not even attempting to better its situation. He then tells her that realism implies, besides truth of detail, the truthful reproduction of typical characters under typical circumstances. Literature, says Engels, is not politically prescriptive; instead it illustrates normal human beings in normal surroundings. In his opinion Miss Harkness has produced a "naturalist" rather than a realistic work because she neglected to show the working class as having a definite historical role or an achievable opportunity to develop its potential.

Engels's letters, taken as one unit, affirm that fiction does not adhere to a definite political commitment since any true realist work dramatizes salient forces of social life. In this particular letter to Miss Harkness Engels further stipulates that a good writer does not encumber his work with his own political views because once he reveals, objectively, the real or possible factors at work in a situation, then he is already taking a political stand. In *The Holy Family* (1845) Marx further clarifies his ideological position regarding reality in art. In it he levels criticism at Eugene Sue's novel titled *The Mysteries of Paris* (1844). He makes his point by taking Fleur de Marie, one of the principal protagonists, as an example of his concept of realism in literature. He says:

> [...] She (Fleur de Marie) is *good* because she has never caused *suffering* to anybody, she has always been *human* to her inhuman surroundings. She is *good* because ...she is still young, full of hope and vitality. Her situation is *not good* because [...] it is not the expression of her human impulses, the fulfillment of her human desires; because it is full of torment and void of pleasure. She measures her situation in life by her *own individuality*, her natural essence, not by the ideal of good.
>
> In *natural* surroundings the chains of bourgeois life fall off *Fleur de Marie* [...] In her unhappy situation in life she was able to become a lovable, human individual; in her exterior debasement she was conscious that her *human* essence was *her true essence*. Now the filth of modern society which has come into exterior contact with her becomes her innermost being; continual hypochondriac self-torture because of that filth will be her duty, the task of her life appointed by God himself, the self-aim of her existence (Baxandall and Morawski, p. 133).

Marx asserts that realism in a novel can be portrayed as multi-faceted and that it depicts a contradiction between what the characters say and what they do, between what they actually are and what they appear or are forced to be. Sue's fiction exemplifies the distinction between the clear social reality that the text demonstrates and the actual "message" it discloses. Reality for Marx encompasses the cognitive value of an artwork. Its authenticity can only be achieved and evaluated by the expression of a recognizable entity such as the dominant traits of a specific social environment in a particular time and location. Linked to the Marxist concept of realism is that of tendency literature. As Baxandall notes, "Tendency" writing or tendentiousness was a phenomenon of the 1840's in Germany. He claims it was also known as "rebel" writing and "committed" literature and defines tendency writing as generally politicized art whose specific aim is to provoke and depict strife against the ruling established order that governs a society. Baxandall warns us that although Marx believed in this type of writing, we must clearly differentiate between Marx's and Lenin's philosophy of tendency writing: Lenin strongly advocated party spirited literature, what he called "*partignost*" (Party Spirit). He believed that literature portrays only the views of the party in power and any divergence from this would result in censure.

Baxandall suggests that although Marx wished artists would understand the working man and his party, he was more concerned with theme, character and setting and with the possible appearance of the artist in his work. Nowhere in his writing does Marx advocate the need for or the likelihood of a proletarian art. Both he and Engels believed that the artist is free to create but, at the same time, also has a responsibility to the nation, to the society and to humanity. They placed great value on the uniqueness of style and, unlike Lenin, affirmed that literature and art are not confined to party rules and restrictions.

Arvon further clarifies Marx's ideology on the projection of reality by the writer when he (Arvon) states that it is the duty of the artist and the writer to side with those men whom Marx describes in the *Communist Manifesto* (1848) as:

> bringing to light and ensuring in the various national struggles of the proletariat the triumph of the interests of the proletariat as a whole which are common and independent of nationality, on the one hand, and at the same time consistently representing the interests of the total movement in the different stages of evolution of the struggle between the proletariat and the bourgeoisie (Arvon, p. 39).

In this manner Marx asserts that reality is representative of the struggle taking place between the proletariat and the bourgeosie but he does not advocate the subsequent Leninist position that art and literature are wholly representative of the party in power.

Arvon confirms this when he says that Marxist esthetics deciphers the innate significance of a class within a totality which encompasses the past, present and future experiences of this class. This type of esthetics, says Arvon, leads to a Socialist humanism whose guiding principle is the search for the essence of humanity. Arvon further states that such a Marxist concept of art and literature places no limitations on writers who may profess different political beliefs; however it does demand that the writer be capable of practicing and writing about an ideological belief that may be at odds with his personal ideology. George Lukács further clarified this Marxist view of the function of the writer in a socialist society when he notes:

> When the artistic development inherent in the situations and the characters imagined by the great realists runs counter to their own cherished biases, and even their most intimate convictions, they do not hesitate for an instant to abandon these biases and convictions and describe what they really see. This cruelty towards their own image of the immediate subjective world constitutes the most profound professional morality of the great realists, as opposed to those minor writers who almost always succeed in reconciling their own vision of the world with reality (quoted in Arvon, p.40)

Marxist esthetic stresses that a great writer rises above his petty political inclinations and portrays reality as it is occurring in the socialist environment that he is depicting in his work of art. From the Marxist perspective, art is not merely an instrument of propaganda.

Another dominant characteristic of Marxist esthetics is its clear opposition to the doctrine of "art for art's sake." Both Marx and Engels asserted that literature and other esthetic phenomena are produced in a context of socio-historical process, and are an essential part of a total activity which allows man to achieve his inborn potential. Literature is dependent on other cultural, social, religious or political activities. Ideologies that are complex would therefore originate from the complexities of a class-divided society. Both Marx and Engels state their objection to "art for art's" sake when they declare:

> The production of ideas, concepts, and the consciousness is first of all directly interwoven with the material activity and the material

intercourse of man, the language of real life. Conceiving, thinking, the spiritual intercourse of men, appear here as the direct efflux of men's material behaviour. The same is true of intellectual production, as it appears in the language of the politics, the laws, the morals, the religion, the metaphysics and so on, of a people. Human beings are the producers of this concept, ideas and so on, that is, real, functioning men, as they are determined by a particular development of their productive forces and of the intercourse corresponding to these forces in its highest form (Demetz, p.65).

Both Marx and Engels assert that art and literature are phenomena that arise from a direct dialectical relationship between man and his environment. Human beings produce a variety of concepts as they interact with their environment. Esthetic sensibilities grow out of this relationship and are also largely determined by it.

An important aspect of Marx's opposition to the philosophy of "art for art's sake" has to be noted here. Marx did not mean that in evaluating a work of art the critic only considers the realistic portrayal of the particular society that the writer makes. He believed that good literature has to consider the imagery, literary devices, use of language, and cadence that the writer employs to describe his content. Marxist literary theory does not deny a non-utilitarian characteristic to the literary phenomenon; however, it strongly adheres to the concept that art is based on the social texture of man and man's works. Marx asserts that since man's nature is irrevocably social, then there can exist no such thing as "pure" art, in the sense of art that is not anchored in any social praxis. He declares that this is particularly true in a non-communist society where class structure still predominates.

In conclusion, it is clear that the critics of Marxist literary theory cited above believe that Marxist esthetics affirms that the writer conveys his ideas through the use of lively images which, because of their particular artistic techniques, produce a reactive impact on the consciousness and literary sentiments of the readers. The Marxist writer, as defined by Arvon and other critics cited above, combines a profound degree of content with lofty ideals to depict genuine human passions and character. To paraphrase the above-mentioned critics, the Marxist writer demonstrates in his work a progressive world outlook in conjunction with progressive ideas based on relevant topical situations. Arvon further implies that while Marxist literary theory states that the major criterion of a work of art is its faithful reflection of a   particular society, it does not eschew the author, his ideology and his personal literary skill; on the contrary, he suggests, Marxist literary theory gives the writer equal importance as the social and historical factors which influenced him in shaping his product.

Chapter 2

A Marxist Reading of Vargas Llosa's La Casa Verde

In *The Green House*[1] Vargas Llosa combines myth with reality to expose the destructive effects that national and international monopoly capitalism have on an uninformed society. The protagonists in this novel include both the people whose livelihood is dictated by the "boom and bust" cycle of the local and foreign corporations, and those who administrate these corporations.

From a more general perspective, the protagonist is also the country of Perú as personified by the towns of Piura, Iquitos and Santa María de Nieva. These towns are political and social microcosms which are representative of the devastating effects that unbridled exploitation of the natural resources have on the country as a whole; one symbol of these destructive effects is the construction of a brothel in Piura by Don Anselmo. The economic survival of this house of prostitution (the "green house"), is proportionally linked to the profitable cultivation and exportation of cotton and hence to the fluctuating levels of prosperity rendered on the town by the sale of this product. The existence of this house of prostitution is therefore symptomatic of the existence of other negative spread effects caused by the false prosperity that results from the spread of unchecked monopoly capitalism in Perú.

In *The Green House* the writer also portrays the destructive impact that unrestrained exploitation (misnamed progress) has on the native Indian ecosystem, as exemplified by the plight of the Indian Jum. The plot encompasses separate (Iquitos and Piura) but interrelated parts and is unravelled against a backdrop of verifiable historical occurrences consisting mainly of events that occurred at the beginning of the twentieth century and those which happened between World War 2 and the present. It is these historical events that will be used as a starting point in a Marxist literary analysis of this novel.

An effective point of departure in this part of this analysis is an examination of the relationship between the existence of real environmental elements and fictional elements described in the novel. In his *Historia Secreta de una Novela* (1971) Vargas Llosa describes the existence of an actual "Casa Verde" in Piura and also provides ample evidence of the existence of la Mangachería and of other environmental locations mentioned in the novel. He says:

> [...] Cuando partí de Piura a Lima, en el verano de 1946, llevaba la cabeza constelada de imágenes...Dos de ellas cobraron cada día más peso y más vida, y se convirtieron en dos inseparables compañeras, en dos secretos mitos. La primera era la silueta de una casa erguida en las afueras de Piura [...] solitaria entre los médanos de arena. La casa ejercía una atracción fascinante sobre mis compañeros y sobre mí. Era una construcción rústica, una choza más que una casa, y había sido enteramente pintada de verde. Todo era extraño en ella: el hecho de estar tan apartada de la ciudad, su inesperado color [...] Había algo maligno y enigmático, un relente diabólico alrededor de esta vivienda a la que habíamos bautizado "la casa verde". Nos habían prohibido acercarnos a ella [...] Lo verdaderamente divertido era observar "la casa verde" de noche [...] Podíamos ver las luces, podíamos escuchar la música [...] Apenas caían las sombras sobre Piura,"la casa verde" empezaba a recibir muchas visitas, y, curiosamente, sólo masculinas.[2]

The Marxist literary theory that stipulates that literature is situated on a verifiable and cognitive entity is verified by the author's testimony to the actual existence of this bordello in Piura. This Marxist insistence on the faithful reproduction of empirical detail in a work of art is further observed in the novel when the author mentions his actual subsequent visit to the "green house." He notes in *Historia Secreta*...:

> Así conocí "la casa verde" por dentro [...] Confieso que tuve una cierta desilusión [...] Las señoras parecían menos orgullosas, menos altas, menos elegantes, más folklóricas y vulgares que siete años

atrás...[el burdel] consistía en una sóla habitación, llena de puertas que daban al desierto. Había una orquesta de tres hombres: un viejo casi ciego que tocaba el arpa, un guitarrista y cantor que era muy joven, y una especie de gigante, levantador de pesas o luchador profesional, que manipulaba el tambor y los platillos [...] Y entre el bar y la orquesta estaban las habitantas, caminando de un lado a otro o fumando sentados en toscas banquetas apoyadas contra la pared, en espera de los nocturnos visitantes. Estos llegaban con las sombras, y [...] Luego las parejas salían a celebrar sus ceremonias en la arena, al pie de los médanos, bajo las fosforescentes estrellas norteñas. En esto consistía [...] todo el misterio de "la casa verde" (Vargas Llosa, pp.20-22)

The documentation of the actual existence of the "green house" serves as the basis for the narration of the lives of the people in the text. The description of the existence of these environmental factors by the writer offers strong support to the Marxist aspect of literary theory that states that literature is anchored in real situations.

A third example of the realistic reproduction of the environment in the novel is contained in Vargas Llosa's description of one of the slum areas known in the narrative and in actual life as la Mangachería. In the novel this "barrio" was instrumental in the formation of the character of some of the personalities described in the novel. About la Mangachería Vargas Llosa says in *Historia Secreta*...:

El barrio se llamaba la Mangachería. Vivía en él gente muy pobre, y la mayoría de sus casas eran frágiles cabañas de barro y caña brava, erguidas en la arena, porque la Mangachería se hallaba también en el desierto, exactamente en el ángulo de la ciudad opuesto al de "la casa verde." Este barrio miserable era el más alegre y el más original de Piura. En muchas de sus chozas un asta rústica hacía flamear banderillas rojas o blancas sobre los techos; es decir, eran chicherías y picanterías donde se podían beber todas las variedades de la chicha, desde el clarito hasta la más espesa, y gustar los innumerables platos de la cocina local. Todos los conjuntos musicales, todas las orquestas piruanas habían nacido en la Mangachería. Los mejores guitarristas, los mejores arpistas, los mejores compositores de valses y tonderos y los mejores cantantes de la ciudad eran mangaches (Vargas Llosa, pp. 15-16).

A fourth element in *La Casa Verde* that supports this Marxist literary concept can be seen in the description Vargas Llosa makes of the effects of foreign exploitation in Iquitos and Piura. In her text, *Dependency Theory and Literary analysis: Reflections on Vargas Llosa's The Green House*[3], M. J. Fenwick coherently documents the actual historical exploitation of Piura and Iquitos by foreign and foreign-dominated corporations. The following paraphrase from her text clearly demonstrates the methodological exploitation of these regions in Perú (and of Perú as a whole) by these foreign companies during the time mentioned in the novel.

Fenwick argues that foreign capitalist investment and exploitation began in the second half of the nineteenth century in Perú. This exploitation was carried out both by the Europeans and by the Americans, with England being the dominant exploiter until after World War 1, when the U.S. assumed more influence and control. The world demand for rubber during the first World War prompted the arrival of joint British and U.S. companies as far west into the Peruvian Amazon as Iquitos. The Booth Steamship Company of London and Liverpool was operating from Liverpool to Manaos to Iquitos. The principal company that supplied the raw material that was sold to the foreign market was The Peruvian Amazon Company started by Julio Arana, a Peruvian.

Fenwick further states that Arana, who dissolved his business relationship with the U.S. in favor of a relationship with the British, managed to establish a rubber monopoly in Iquitos between 1904-1905. She suggests that Arana's monopoly had the following effects: one, it gained for Perú the territory between it and Colombia; two, it put an end to the intention of U.S. firms to build railroads into Iquitos and three, it assured the British an economic foothold in the rubber being produced there. She further says that the principal source of Arana's labor force came from the jungle Indians who lived in the area. This labor pool was divided into one group (the Indians) who realized the actual production process and a second group (foreigners) who supervised the Indian laborers and trained other workers. This second group was also responsible for killing those (Indians) who tried to defect. According to Fenwick:

> The Indians from the Iquitos-Amazon area were brought by the Peruvian Amazon Company from the villages to the area being exploited, were housed in large warehouses, were overworked,

starved and beaten on the theory that it was more profitable to replace them than to care for them. The consensus was that the Indian population fell in five years from 50,000 to 8,000 as a result of the rubber company's slave massacres. This activity which destroyed 80% of the male Indian population at the same time destroyed the labor force for the agricultural production essential to the survival of the Indian villages (Fenwick, p. 57).

Fenwick asserts that by 1910 Asian rubber became available to Britain and to the U.S. at a cheaper price because the British had smuggled rubber seedlings into Malaya and Ceylon from Perú. For the British especially, the product was cheaper because these colonies were part of its empire and the transportation from them to Britain was cheaper and faster. The supply of cheaper rubber prompted the British, at the start of the First World War, to abandon the Amazon companies (like Arana's) in favor of Asian rubber. These companies went bankrupt and the effect on the society was devastating.

During this "boom" period the exploitation of rubber had an enormous impact on the town of Iquitos. By 1896 the population of this town had swollen as people migrated here in hopes of securing employment. The economic base had switched from subsistence agriculture to export agriculture (rubber), and its culture had changed to reflect a craving for foreign products. For example:

[...] A street was paved with Portuguese tiles, houses were built of imported materials (one was designed by Eiffel of Paris), and the new Peruvian bourgeoisie like Julio Arana as well as the foreigners wore imported clothing and drank imported wines (Fenwick, p. 58).

In the novel Vargas Llosa closely adheres to this historical data. For example, Fenwick suggests that in the narrative Julio's father represents this early period since he is apparently a rubber baron much like Arana. Like his son, Julio's father lost his fortune when the British abandoned the Amazon companies in favor of the cheaper Asian product.

During the Second World War, the Europeans were denied the supply of Asian rubber and they returned to Perú for the rubber which was essential in the manufacture of tanks, airplanes and other equipment utilized for the defense of Allied territories. Fenwick states that the U.S., after it entered the war, signed a contract for all of Perú's rubber in exchange for twenty five million dollars, to be used for the development of Perú's agriculture and industry. After the war, synthetic rubber became popular and cheaper and the economy of Iquitos was again negatively affected by the needs of the foreign markets. The industrial growth for which the twenty five million dollars was earmarked was never carried out in the Amazon area. The cultivation of rubber in Iquitos during the "boom" caused by World War 2 was different from the method of cultivation practiced before. Fenwick summarizes this difference in this manner:

> During the World War II rubber boom in the Iquitos-Amazon area there were significant changes in the means of production. This time the labor force basic to production (although still Indian) was not kept in strict slavery or transported out of the community but was forced to gather the rubber from the immediate area. The structure of the Indian communities was basically kept together but segregated from the dominant structure. Of course a serious internal change resulted from the fact that a large part of the workers' total labor time was taken away from agricultural production and was put into supplying rubber to the intermediaries. Their pay was not based on a salary-money arrangement but was merchandise trade (Fenwick, p. 59).

This change in the mode of production and cultivation of rubber affected the society in two ways: First, the indians had less time to devote to the cultivation of the agricultural products necessary for survival. Secondly, it divided the society into hierarchical classes which segregated the indians from the rest of the population since it relegated them to the bottom of the social pyramid.

According to the novel, during the "bust" period, Julio Reátegui, an Iquitos businessman, produced wood and coffee when the demand for rubber was not high. However, as soon as the demand for rubber increased during the World War 2 period, Julio was able to re-establish his father's business. In addition, since the U.S. had agreed to purchase all of Peruvian rubber, then the contraband rubber trade flourished as people tried to sell rubber to the Japanese.

In the novel, Reátegui and Fushía obtained their labor force from the Aguaruna and Huambisa Indian tribes. These Indians were not "warehoused" as before, and they were also paid in merchandise rather than cash. Vargas Llosa therefore inculcates real historical events in his narrative: Julio's workers are prototypes of the actual laborers who worked for the foreign companies and in the novel they are treated in the same manner as the actual laborers were. The writer produces a close correlation between verifiable historical occurrences and the literary events in the text. The credibility of the protagonists and of the novel is seemingly enhanced by the authenticity of historical details which serve as the environment in which these characters function. As Fenwick asserts:

> The labor source in the novel for Reátegui and Fushía's illegal rubber market was from the Aguaruna and Huambisa Indian villages. The narrative seems to be an accurate elaboration of the historical data in that the tribes were not herded away like in the earlier decades of rubber production; they gathered rubber in their own areas, traded with intermediaries, were paid in merchandise instead of wages, and they maintained their traditional community organization interrupted only in that they worked for the capitalist enterprise (Fenwick, p.60).

Vargas Llosa therefore successfully utilizes aspects of a historical reality to increase the credibility of his protagonists and through them, of the novel. This literary technique has the added effect of making his social criticism more logical and credible. He accurately elaborates historical data and intertwines it with mythical (but representative) characters to describe the negative effects caused by an entrenched capitalist economy. Vargas Llosa projects a Marxist reality in the text as he combines myth (Julio) with reality (the documented treatment of the Indians) to convincingly describe the devastating social effects caused by uncurbed monopoly capitalism and an unrefrained monoculture.

Another manner through which the Marxist definition of reality in a novel is presented in *The Green House* is through the description of Piura and its environs. Fenwick stresses that the historical references made to this area are accurate and detailed. For instance, she notes that cotton became the primary product here in response to U.S. demand as early as 1860-64 during the American Civil War. During these war years when U.S. cotton was not available, Peruvian cotton was sold to the British.

However after the American Civil War she notes that U.S. cotton was produced and marketed worldwide and this caused a decrease in the demand and price of Peruvian cotton. This "boom and bust" economic cycle resulted in that Perú had to use the land previously held for cotton production for the cultivation of other products. By 1900 the foreign market once more demanded Peruvian cotton and once again the land in Piura was utilized for its production. This exploitation of the land was so intense that there was large scale foreign investment in irrigation and machinery and: "By 1908 cotton production was 30% of the total national export and was replacing the crops more essential to Peruvian food consumption..."(Fenwick, p.63). This exploitation of the resources by a foreign corporation and this deliberate creation of a monoculture to satisfy the needs of foreign countries were patterns of economic exploitation which were concurrently established, both in Iquitos and in Piura. In the novel the writer projects these historical realities by demonstrating the negative effects that the cultivation of cotton and rubber had on the society of Piura and Iquitos. The protagonists in each of the two towns function in an economic environment created by the exploitation of a monoculture. Their lives and economic well-being are dictated by the economic needs of a foreign country and this results in that they have little or no control over their financial destiny. By 1912 the U.S. became involved in this exploitation of cotton through the investment of a U.S. owned corporation called W.R.Grace and Company and by 1920, Fenwick states that this company was producing five-eighths of Perú's cotton and shipping it to U.S. markets on its own boats.

This export-import company had also invested heavily in sugar production in Perú and sold products originating from foreign countries in the Peruvian market. Vargas Llosa identifies some of these products in the novel as cars, champagne, and clothing. The prosperity of Piura during this period prompted Don Anselmo to successfully operate the first "green house." Vargas Llosa utilizes an empirically verifiable accomplishment as the ambience in which Don Anselmo functions and as the entity which directly prompted the establishment of this house of prostitution.

Fenwick suggests that by the end of the First World War, the cultivation of cotton was mechanized, and this mechanization led to widespread unemployment. In the novel one of the results of this pattern of unemployment was the growth of slum areas such as la

Mangachería and Gallinacera. The change in the mode of production had several other effects, one of which was the partial restructuring of the existing social class, resulting in the creation of a distinct culture and way of life by this slum dwellers who in the novel consider themselves primarily Piurans rather than Peruvians.

Finally, in demonstrating the Marxist perspective of literary reality in *The Green House*, it is necessary to examine the names of characters in the novel and assess whether or not they reflect actual personalities who may or may not have existed during the periods covered by the narrative. In *Mario Vargas Llosa: La Invención de una Realidad* (1970), José Miguel Oviedo asserts that a considerable portion of *The Green House* is based on real events. He states:

> [...] Existieron en Piura, como hemos visto, un burdel de color verde y los músicos de su pobre orquesta, con los mismos nombres con que aparecen en la novela; existió también un Padre García, párroco de origen español; los Seminarios son en Piura una familia enorme y poderosa, casi el sinónimo de la ciudad; el crecimiento y desaparición de la mangachería es parte del desarollo urbano de la costa, etc...[4]

Vargas Llosa utilized not only actual historical events in the novel but also distinct names of existing personalities. For example, Señor Seminario is the name given in the novel to the man that Lituma killed. Mario Vargas Llosa himself supports the use of real names in the novel when he writes in *Crónica de un Viaje a la Selva* (1958) :

> La primera referencia concreta que tuve acerca de algún patrón [para *La Casa Verde*] fue en Chicais. Allí se nos habló de uno de ellos, muy famoso, que parece extraído de una novela macabre. Se llama Tushía-de origen japonés-y vive en el río Santiago, donde posee una isla. En esa región inaccesible, Tushía reina como un señor feudal. Tiene un harén para su uso, compuesto de numerosas mujeres (once nos dijeron), la mayoría de las cuales habían sido arrebatados por sus matones a los pueblos aguarunas o huambisas. Una de estas mujeres (una niña de 12 años) había huido de la isla y acababa de pasar por Chicais cuando nosotros estuvimos allí (Quoted from Oviedo, p.156).

The writer's historical knowledge of Esther Chuwik seems to be a blueprint for his description of Bonifacia in the novel. About Esther, the novelist says:

Esther Chuwik es una niña de unos diez años. Es alta, frágil, de ojos claros y voz suave. Conversamos con ella después de la actuación escolar. Esta niña, como otras niñas de la selva, fue raptada tres años atrás. Sus raptores la llevaron primero a Chiclayo y luego a Lima, donde se le utilizaba como sirvienta [...] El rapto de niños es frecuente en la selva. Sólo en Chicais se han constatado 29 raptos. Los patrones, los ingenieros que hacen trabajos de exploración en el interior de la Amazonia, los oficiales de las guarniciones e incluso los misioneros suelen llevarse una niña para dedicarla a las labores domésticas. Algunas se llevan varias, para regalarlas a sus amigos. Esto me hubiera parecido, si alguien me lo hubiera contado, demasiado monstruoso para creerlo (Quoted from Oviedo, p.156).

Again we perceive that the novelist's account of the kidnapping of Bonifacia in the novel was based on real events and on his acquaintance with Esther Chuwik.

In the same account [*Crónica de un viaje a la selva*] the author recounts the inhuman methods used by the Mission to capture and kidnap pupils for the school. His account is very similar to the descriptions of the same practice that he elaborates in the novel. In the *Crónica* he states:

En Urakusa, algunos meses atrás, Morote Best (antropólogo peruano que acompañaba al autor en el viaje), por ejemplo, consiguió rescatar a dos niñas separadas por este arbitrario sistema de su pueblo. He visto las fotos, tomadas en aquella oportunidad por Morote: sobre una lancha se ven dos monjas de rostro taciturno, rodeadas de soldados y, a su lado, dos niñas raptadas (Oviedo, p.156)

This description by the novelist coincides directly with the opening scene of *The Green House*. In this particular instance the narrator employed a direct aspect of historical reality to concretize the narrative on historical and realistic events.

Perhaps the most faithful reproduction of real personalities that the author employs in the novel is the detailed description of Jum's rebellion. In *Mario Vargas Llosa: La invención...* José Miguel Oviedo describes this incident in this fashion:

> Quizá porque la historia era la más cruel de todas, Vargas Llosa quiso tratarla con máxima objetivedad (sin traicionar el clima general de la novela, sin demagogias) y conservó para dejar constancia de su escándalo, los nombres propios implicados en el hecho. En su detallada crónica, figura "un cabo de la guarnición de Borja, llamado Roberto Delgado Campos como promotor del incidente en el pueblo Urakusa;" el encuentro de Jum y el Gobernador de Santa María de Nieva; la represión policial contra el pueblo; el martirio de Jum y, finalmente, su acta de acusación contra los culpables: "los autores materiales de este acto demoníaco son: el Teniente Gobernador de Santa María de Nieva, Julio Reátegui; el Juez de Paz, Arévalo Benzas; el alcalde Manuel Aguila, y el Teniente del Batallón de Ingenieros número cinco, Ernesto Bohórquez Rojas" (Oviedo, p.157).

The preservation of real names in the narrative directly supports the Marxist aspect of literary theory that states that literature is based on a realistic portrayal of circumstances, events and personalities.

The personalities of *The Green House* are extrapolated in great part from a reality which Vargas Llosa himself describes as painful. The narrative appears as fiction but we know that this fiction nurtures itself from reality. The work seems to be irreality extracted from reality or, to put it differently, myth combined with truth. This combination of fiction and historically verifiable events makes the novel more authentic. Vargas Llosa describes this portrayal of reality in the novel in this manner:

> Las mejores novelas son siempre las que agotan su materia, las que no dan una sola luz sobre la realidad, sino muchas [...] Las novelas de caballerías dan soberbias representaciones de su tiempo. Abarcan la realidad en su nivel mítico, en su nivel religioso, en su nivel histórico, en su nivel social, en su nivel instintivo. Ha habido una especie de decadencia de la novela en los últimos tiempos, una especie de repliegue. Las tentativas modernas de la novela quieren dar una visión de un solo canal, de un solo nivel de realidad. Yo estoy, al contrario, por la novela totalizadora, que ambiciona abrazar una realidad en todas sus fases, en todas sus manifestaciones. No puede hacerse nunca en todas. Pero, mientras más fases consiga dar,

la visión de la realidad será más amplia y la novela será más completa (Quoted in Oviedo, p.67).

Another characteristic of Marxist literary theory that will be used in the analysis of this novel is Marx's assertion of the proportional relationship between the economic base and the superstructure.

The novel describes the life of the people of both Iquitos and Piura and shows how it was affected by the production of rubber in the former and cotton in the latter. Although these towns were separated by geography, they shared a common bond of national and international exploitation. The rubber industry in Iquitos was, as we now know, exploited by the Booth Steamship Company of London and Liverpool and the cultivation and exportation of cotton in Piura was realized by W.R.Grace and company, a U.S. owned corporation. We will now discuss the relationship between the economic base and the hierarchical social superstructure as it occurred in Iquitos.

In this town the economic base stratified the society into three separate but interrelated sections, identified by Fenwick as the wealthy financiers, the intermediaries and the common laborers. The economic level and social position of members of each of these sections is proportional to its degree of dependency on the economic base. Hence their very existence is directly dependent on the production, cultivation and marketing of rubber.

At the top of the social pyramid in Iquitos are the rich capitalists exemplified by people like Julio Reátegui and Don Fabio Cuesta. Both finance the production of rubber and exploit the labor of others for their own profits. Julio is a prime example of how the fluctuating economic base directly reflects the social and economic niche of the individual. His business and profits increase or decrease in accordance with the foreign need for rubber. Although he appears to be his own boss, he is in reality only a link in the chain of economic exploitation. He serves in the novel as one of the rubber entrepreneurs who sees that the product is cultivated and taken to Lima and from there to the exterior.

Reátegui, like all the other inhabitants of Iquitos, has no control over the actual price of the rubber and has no concept of the size of the profits realized by the foreign corporation. His profits are instead dictated by the fluctuating price of the product, whose market price is set by the international company.

Reátegui's wealth gives him political connections as well as power. He becomes the titular governor of Santa María, and appoints his crony Cuesta to run the town while he manages his other more lucrative businesses. The economic base in Iquitos allows Reátegui to occupy a prominent position in the society and to dictate the financial and social welfare of others lower in the exploitative chain. The wealth which he garners from both the legal and contraband sale of rubber enables him to purchase other businesses and to possess other fancy accoutrements that only the rich could afford. For example, his wealth allows him to travel and to buy imported goods for his consumption. It also provides him with strong political ties in the capital which permits his illegal rubber trade with the Axis to go unpunished. As Fenwick notes:

> [...] These men (Julio Reátegui and Fabio Cuesta) are in the position to determine the economic and class position of those lower in the hierarchy and manipulate their labor relations. Since they monopolize the Iquitos outlet for raw materials, they are able to curtail any independent actions on the part of the intermediaries, and furthermore they have dehumanized the Indian's culture and labor to the extent that their use in the society is as human commodities.
>
> Reátegui is the primary rubber "boss" in the Amazon area with headquarters in Iquitos. His family had profited from the earlier rubber boom, and don Julio was able to reestablish the capital investment when the new war demanded more rubber from the area Reátegui owned warehouses, a sawmill, and a hotel in Iquitos, was governor of Santa María, and was involved in marketing lumber, rubber, and young Indian women. His dealings were with traders- both legal and illegal, bandits, banks, the Catholic mission, and the national government in Lima. His social life as well was connected with the ruling sector in Lima, and he made occasional trips there for national cultural celebrations (Fenwick, p.41).

The high social and economic position that the cultivation and sale of rubber afforded Julio exemplifies the dialectical relationship between the economic base and the superstructure. The marketing of this product enabled him to negatively affect the lives of the Indian laborers and, at the same time, enhance his social position in Iquitos. His control of the export of rubber to the capital allows Julio to effectively truncate any other economic ambitions exhibited by the intermediaries (like Fushía) who brought him the rubber from the interior, and enables him to to dictate the lives of others lower in the exploitative economic chain. Julio's livelihood was therefore directly linked to the exploitation of the economic base (rubber) and his fortunes fluctuated in accordance with the world demand for this product.

The other social group in Iquitos directly below Julio's is composed of the intermediaries in the chain of the exploitation of the economic base. Fenwick says that some of these are Nieves, Lituma, Fushía and Aquilino, and their primary function is to deliver the product from the interior to the capitalist financiers like Julio. The economic and social relationship between this group and the productive base (rubber) is more symbiotic than that of Reátegui's. Julio's social position and wealth permits him to diversify to other business enterprises. This diversification allows him a small measure of independence from the economic base.

Fushía and the others, however, are unable to embark in a similar business venture since they do not possess enough capital to invest in other enterprises. Even if they had had the capital, their efforts probably would have been stymied by men like Julio who depend on them to deliver the product to Iquitos. Consequently, their economic and social status is totally dependent on the exploitation and sale of rubber.

Fushía for example is a fugitive Japanese-Brazilian who is Julio's middleman in his illegal rubber trade wih the Axis. His economic well-being is determined by the sale of rubber and by the specific needs of Julio. Fushía's niche in the society is directly determined by his function in the chain of exploitation of rubber. By facilitating Reátegui's illegal trade, Fushía is directly instrumental in enhancing Julio's wealth and high social position. When Julio's contraband business dealings are exposed, he craftily manipulates his political connections so that full blame for the illegal rubber trade falls on Fushía.

Fushía, now a fugitive of the Peruvian authorities, has to flee into the interior of the Amazon. Here he sets up his own rubber business with the Indians. He buys their rubber with trinkets and sells it, through Aquilino, to the merchants in the town of Santa María. Unlike Julio, Fushía lacks the capital and the political "strings" to make the business profitable.

In the novel we witness his misfortune as he is discarded by Julio after having served his purpose. His place in society is dictated by his economic status, which is in turn determined by his relationship to the production and sale of rubber. As an intermediary, he achieves some measure of success; however, as an independent businessman he fails totally since he lacks the capital and the powerful political friends that are necessary for him to run a successful business. Fushía's relationship to the economic base is not profitable for him. He has no concept of the real price of the exploited product and his meagre profits are set by the capitalist merchants like Julio. He is presented as having no other means of livelihood and as subject to the whims and the needs of a foreign market, as represented by Julio. Fushía's life clearly supports the Marxist theory that the economic base directly affects aspects of the superstructure.

As an intermediary, the hierarchical position (economic and social) of Fushía is directly linked to the fluctuating profits generated by the sale of rubber.

In Iquitos the Indians occupy the lowest rung in the social hierarchy. Their economic and social position is also dictated by their relationship to the economic base and they represent the group that is greater in number and that is the victim of exploitation by members of each of the other two social strata. Their labor is exploited by people like Fushía who pay them in trinkets for their rubber. Indirectly, they are the victims of exploitation by the merchants like Julio who ultimately depend on them for the steady supply of rubber. They are forced to work for the capitalists and Indians who escape the labor camp, are hunted down by the army, and killed. They are not allowed to form any sort of labor unions or co-operatives. When Jum attempts to convince his fellow Indians that they would be better off if they bypassed the intermediaries and sold the rubber directly to the city merchants, he is captured and tortured by the army. Their economic well-being and their very own lives are dependent on the exploitation of the economic base.

The Indians had no control over the distribution and sale of the product and they are not even paid in cash. Fenwick describes their place in the social hierarchy in the following manner:

> [...] The Indian men in the novel have a relationship to the means of production that is determined by the White "bosses." They are forced to sell their labor gathering rubber in the area they inhabit...They are forced to produce by penalty of physical punishment. They have no control over the market price received for the rubber or other natural resources nor over the process of distribution. Jum and the other Indian workers provide an essential part of the labor for the national economic activity, but in exchange for their labor they are given beads and trinkets, and are thus kept from participating in the dominant system of money exchange or in the dominant culture. Neither did Jum or the Indians speak Spanish except for the few words they picked up from the trade relationships, like "limagovernment" and "shit, government flag" (Fenwick, p.38).

When the demand for rubber was high, Indian labor was intensely exploited. However, when the market price dropped, then their labor was no longer needed and they were no longer "warehoused" to ensure a constant pool of laborers.

The treatment that the Indians in the novel received can be compared to the manner in which they were treated by the Spaniards during the encomienda system in the early sixteenth century. In this system they were forced to work for the Spanish masters for no financial gain. Similarly, the exploitation of rubber by the foreign companies in the twentieth century also directly results in the Indians (like Jum) being forced to work for no pay and being hunted, killed and tortured if they fled to evade work. The economic fate of the Indians is totally linked to the exploitation of the economic base; by the same token, their position in the social scale is dictated entirely by their relation to the exploitation of rubber. Since they are simple laborers, then they are relegated to the very bottom of the social pyramid and are treated as objects rather than people.

This practice destroys the Indians's traditional way of life as it detracts them from cultivating their necessary agricultural products. Because they are unable to produce the essential food products indispensable for their subsistence, then they have to buy them. For the Indians this becomes a frustrating vicious circle: they have to work in the production of rubber to be able to obtain food to subsist. Since they are not paid in cash, then they have to trade their rubber for canned goods from people like Fushía and Aquilino. As the price of these canned goods was set by the intermediaries like Fushía, then the Indians find themselves cultivating increasingly more rubber to exchange for the same or for a lesser amount of canned goods.

This intensification of the cultivation process results in less time to plant subsistence agricultural products and subsequently increases their dependency on foodstuff that is bartered for their rubber. As is economically logical, this vicious circle is directly propagated by men like Aquilino and Fushía, by the rich merchants like Julio, and ultimately by the foreign corporations like the Booth Steamship Company.

For the Indians there seems to be no way out of this economic trap. In the novel they are shown as vainly attempting to function in a situation which they did not create and over which they have no control. Jum, for example, tries to form co-operatives that would have allowed them to sell their product directly to the city merchants and therefore reap a profit in cash. Because of this attempt, he is hunted and tortured by the army which protects the interests of the wealthy. The Indians are forced to be unwilling participants in a capitalist system for which they are not culturally prepared. Since they are the common laborers, then they are relegated to the bottom of the hierarchy and their niche in the economic and social strata is wholly determined by their relationship to the economic base.

The novel points out that in Piura cotton is the principal economic base. New highways and railroads indicate the importance of this export and are symptomatic of the town's apparent prosperity. However, the city has also acquired the symptoms of poverty in the form of a slum sector called la Mangachería. (Fenwick attributes this phenomenon to mechanization of the cultivation of cotton). Like Iquitos, Piura produces cotton primarily for an export market and its level of prosperity fluctuates in accordance with the needs of a foreign market.

This production for an export market also makes the economic base in Piura the sole determiner of the superstructure. The cultivation and sale of cotton has created a distinct compartmentalization of the society into a rigid class structure which is determined by the individual's relationship to the means of production. This class structure stratifies the society into three separate groups, each of which depends on the production and sale of cotton for its economic and social survival. Fenwick identifies each of these three groups in Piura in the following manner:

[...] In the Piura area are 1) the unemployed or underemployed slum residents who participate only marginally in the labor market, 2) the group which aspires to some degree of social mobility in the military, the Church, or as manager or owner of a small business, and 3) the landowners who control the production process and the economy through implicit alliances with the national government. (Fenwick, pp. 37-38)

At the top of the social ladder in Piura are the wealthy landowners (identified as number three in the above quotation) who finance the cultivation of cotton and facilitate its exploitation by multinational concerns. Since the novelist does not dwell on the production process in Piura, then he does not fully develop the personality of any of the members of this group of wealthy landowners. Instead, he mentions representative names like Chápiro Seminario, the Chief of Police and Don Eusebio Romero. The wealth and influence of this elitist group is seen and felt throughout the description of life in Piura. For example, the text suggests that it was the wealth of one or all of these landowners that financed the construction of the original Green House, patronized by the elite of Piura.

This elitist group is able to diversify its finances (like Reátegui in Iquitos) into other businesses, exemplified here by their financial support of the house of prostitution. However, they are able to do this only because they have accumulated enough capital through their control of the means of production, distribution and transportation of the economic base. It is perceived that because this group totally monopolizes the economic base then it can afford to purchase foreign consumer goods (like champagne) for its use and can manipulate the economic future of intermediaries like Don Anselmo. It can then be seen that the economic and social survival of this wealthy group in Piura is directly linked to its symbiotic relationship it enjoys with the economic base.

In descending order, the second social group in Piura (identified as group two in the above quotation) is comprised of people like don Anselmo and La Chunga, his daughter. Don Anselmo comes to Piura when cotton production is at its height and profits are good.

It is strongly suspected that he has the financial backing of a latifundista in the construction of the first Green House. Don Anselmo is then an intermediary (like Fushía) between the capitalists and their business.

Don Anselmo's profits in the Green House are entirely dependent on the wealth generated by the cultivation and sale of cotton. The house of prostitution that he manages is frequented by the police chief and other members of the privileged sector in Piura. Don Anselmo lives by exploiting other human beings. In the actual construction of the Green house he utilizes members of the poorest class in Piura whom he pays with chicha and sugar rather than with cash (we remember that Jum was paid in trinkets rather than cash for his rubber). Don Anselmo also exploits the prostitutes who work for him in the Green House. Again he pays them with bed and board instead of with cash. His business prospers as long as the profits from the exploitation of the economic base are satisfactory.

Don Anselmo's wealth and very livelihood are in this manner linked to the economic prosperity generated by the sale of cotton. As long as this is profitable, then enough people will frequent his business and enrich him and the secret latifundista proprietor of the Green House.

However the moral outrage of the townspeople increases in proportion to the increase of Don Anselmo's economic position. In the novel he compounds the people's dislike of him when he abducts Antonia, a blind deaf-mute whose wealthy parents had been killed by robbers and forces her to live with him in the Green House. Antonia dies of childbirth and Don Anselmo is left to raise a baby girl by himself. Outraged because of the existence of this brothel in their midst and because of his cruel treatment of Antonia, the townspeople, led by Padre García, burn the Green House. Don Anselmo loses his business and his social and economic position in the town. To make a living, he now has to play his harp in the town square for monetary handouts from passersby. In the end he moves into the slums and dies a poor man.

In Don Aselmo's case we again perceive Marx's concept of the proportional relationship between the economic base and the superstructure: his house of prostitution exists because of the prosperity generated in the town by the exploitation of cotton, the economic base. It is patronized by the elite of Piura, who enrich themselves because of their profitable relationship to the economic base. Don Anselmo's subsistence is totally dependent on the money generated by the cultivation and marketing of cotton. Since he has no capital to diversify into other enterprises (like Fushía in Iquitos), then he is left penniless when he is deprived of his only means of subsistence. As a harp player, he sells his services to the rich, who employ him to entertain their guests during their parties. As we know, the wealthy people who occupy the higher social echelon depend on the exploitation of cotton for their wealth. Thus even as a poor harp player Don Anselmo indirectly depends on the economic base for his subsistence.

The inhabitants of the slum area called la Mangachería are at the bottom of the social and economical hierarchy in Piura. This group is represented by the Champs and exemplified by people like Lituma and Josefino.

In la Mangachería a new green house was constructed by La Chunga, Don Anselmo's daughter. This new brothel was not as elegant as the original one and its clientele was composed of inhabitants of the slums, like the Champs, Josefino and Lituma, rather than of members of the elite as before.

Lituma is an exemplary member of this group. While living in Mangachería, he had become a memeber of some popular political parties to better his social status and now joins the army to enhance his social and economic position. As a soldier, he is promoted to sergeant and is sent to the Amazon as part of the group that protects the business interests of the entrepreneurs. Because of his employment, Lituma's function and usefulness are therefore dependent on the profitable exploitation of the production of cotton.

Lituma's stay in the army ends when he is accused of the murder of a rich man (Señor Seminario) and is sent to prison in Lima for ten years. He loses his rank and is discharged from the army. Lituma returns to Mangachería to discover that Bonifacia, his former girlfriend, is now a prostitute at La Chunga's green house and works for Josefino, his friend, who acts as her pimp. Lituma now reverts to his previous behavior and like the other Champs, now spends his time at La Chunga's. He has no visible means of supporting himself and becomes a part of this displaced group. Jobless, this bottom social group finds itself having to accept haphazard and temporary forms of employment (such as the construction of the green house) in exchange for consumer goods like sugar and chicha.

In the novel Vargas Llosa shows us that the economic base of both Iquitos and Piura dictated the particular social and economic divisions of each region. A Marxist reading of the novel not only shows that the economic base determines the superstructure, but also reveals that each group in the social pyramid exploits the group immediately lower in the social and economic strata. For example, Reátegui exploits Fushía and Fushía exploits the indians. The indians, being at the bottom of the social ladder, have no one to exploit and when they attempt to rebel against their exploitation they are brutally suppressed by the army. Similarly, in Piura one can clearly perceive the chain of exploitation brought about by the cultivaton of cotton. The latifundistas, for example, exploit Don Anselmo who exploits the residents of the slums. Like the indians in Iquitos, the slum dwellers have no one to exploit and attempt to survive by selling their labor (and in some cases their bodies) whenever it is needed.

Another concept of Marxist literary theory that will be utilized in an analysis of *The Green House* is Marx's concept of the relationship between form and content in literature. In applying this literary theory to the novel the narrative structure and then the language of the text will be examined to demonstrate that Marx's form/content concept of literary criticism helps the reader better understand *The Green House*.

In the novel, Vargas Llosa describes both the social and economic disruptions inflicted on the people and the country of Perú by unrestrained monopoly capitalism at both the national and international levels. These disruptions which form the content of the narrative are reflected through an intentional inversion of the traditional narrative structure, the form. The writer disrupts the normal chronological order of the conventional novel to mirror the economic and political destabilization that results from the systematic exploitation of rubber and cotton in Iquitos and Piura. In other words, the narrative form has been adapted to reflect the content. Let us take a closer look at this literary phenomenon. A first reading of the novel clearly shows its division into four sections and an epilogue. Fenwick suggests that each of these four chapters contains a few smaller sections which she aptly labels "action scenes." These sequences of scenes describe individual characters as they attempt to cope with their environment and are described in the following manner by Fenwick:

> [...] The sequence is repeated in order from Bonifacia, to Fushía, to Piura and Don Anselmo, to Jum or Corporal Roberto Delgado in the jungle and to the Mangache Champs. This repeated sequence does not pay logical regard to either time or space. A typical section will have Bonifacia at the colony and reminiscing about Iquitos and Lalita, Don Anselmo starting to build the Green House, Corporal Delgado on his way back to his native jungle town, and Lituma back in Mangachería after ten years in the Lima jail. The time span in any section may be fifty years and the action may jump from Santa María to Iquitos, to the rivers in between, and to Piura-Mangachería (Fenwick, p.89).

Vargas Llosa disrupts the traditional chronological order of time, space and action in the novel in order to reflect the quest for self and for identity that the characters undertake. This inversion of the narrative structure of the conventional novel is the author's manner of utilizing the form to reflect the erratic nature of the lives of these characters (content). Their seemingly aimless existence is caused in great part by the indiscriminate exploitation of the rubber and cotton that was realized by the national and foreign corporations.

As Fenwick notes, this exploitation is done haphazardly, with the companies going wherever the product was most easily and readily available, regardless of the environmental or social adjustments that it would cause. These exploiters do not unfold logical, rational plans but simply attack targets of opportunity since they were entirely profit oriented. This lack of rational planning leads directly to disruptions in the social order of both Iquitos and Piura. About this societal disruptions Fenwick says:

> [...] The disruption in the time sequence is metaphoric for the historical development pattern imposed on the interior regions of a nation dependent on external power manipulations. For example the concrete historical references in the novel--the Allies, the Amazon rubber boom, the Piura cotton era etc.--are not presented in any logical, sequential, pattern as they figured in the history of the dominant world powers, but are random in the narration and unrelated to any historical sequence significant to the inhabitants of the two areas. Even though the Peruvians--in all levels of the

socio-economic structure--are affected in their labor relations by these external events, they are denied any real sense of the logic that produced them. The farther the narration moves toward the interior of Perú, the less logic have the events for the inhabitants. The time connection between the Allies and the second Amazon rubber boom is obvious and logical from the perspective of U.S. leaders and investors, for example, who were deeply involved in all phases of world history and economic development, but the two events appeared to the Amazon people (according to the novel) in an obscure, illogical connection because the Peruvians whose labor was vital to the events were denied any direct participation in the whole historical process. As we saw previously, the time sequence of economic development in Perú has been determined by foreign corporations and according to their surplus value indicators. To them, therefore, the time sequence has been perfectly logical. However, for the Peruvians who produce the surplus value, historical time has been seen as irregular periods of boom and bust and seemingly is not at all logical (Fenwick, pp. 89-90).

The economic development of these two regions follows no organized or carefully planned agenda. Instead it is geared to accommodate the needs of a foreign market over which the people have no control. By omitting any visible chronological description of the protagonists, the writer successfully depicts this unplanned economic development in the novel.

Language in *The Green House* is another aspect of the narrative structure that Vargas Llosa utilizes to demonstrate the close correspondence between content and form. In the novel, the author utilizes it to portray the confused and aimless nature of the lives of the personalities he describes. By subdividing the language into stratified hierarchical levels, the novelist ultimately reveals not only the characters of the protagonists but also the different levels of exploitation to which they have been reduced. For example Jum's inability to speak Spanish reflects his incapacity to live comfortably in a capitalistic society. This same handicap is also utilized by the government to further exploit his labor and that of his Indian colleagues. When Jum protests against the treatment meted out to the Indians by the government, the military attempts to pacify him by making him sign a useless piece of paper which they have Jum believe is a treaty. Unable to read and ignorant of the language, Jum does not realize that this "treaty" is only a piece of old newspaper and he signs it. In this example one can clearly perceive the language embodying the content and demonstrating the correlation between content and form: because of the language barrier (the form), Jum (the content) was unable to function in a capitalist-oriented environment. If Jum had possessed the ability to read Spanish he would have quickly become aware of the deceit that the Peruvian government (repesented by the army) was perpatrating on him and on his people. Jum's ignorance of the language was therefore a weapon used further to extend his exploitation and to obtain his labor and his product.

Jum's daughter, Bonifacia, is another example of how language is used in the novel to express the level of exploitation of the people. Like many other Indian girls, Bonifacia was captured and brought to the Catholic Mission at Santa María to be "trained" by the nuns. She was taught Spanish as well as the culture and ethics of the non-Indian population (that is, of the exploiters). Once deemed "trained" by the nuns, she was to be given to the rich families of the town or to the military as a servant. We therefore perceive that Bonifacia's knowledge of the language was the key to her exploitation: because she knew it, she was considered appropriately prepared to serve the privileged class. As in the case of her father Jum, language serves as a means of exploitation. Jum was exploited through lack of knowledge of the language; for Bonifacia, knowledge of the language was the instrument by means of which her labor was exploited.

Carlos Fuentes analyzes this use of the language in *The Green House* when he suggests:

Vargas Llosa corrompe, implacablemente [...] A las jerarquías, opone una delirante confusión verbal en la que el pasado es narrado en presente y el presente en pasado; en la que la coincidencia interna de la situación en la escritura, aunque no en el espacio y en el tiempo, asimila, hermana, revela una condición común patibularia y bastarda, des-jerarquiza a los hombres polares: el bandido Fushía y el probo gobernador Don Julio Reátegui; en la que las formas verbales asumen indiscriminadamente todo el caudal simultáneo del habla y el gesto, a fin de operar esa ruptura de las oposiciones entre cambio y estructura: "Tú pasaron cerca y en caballos chúcaros, que tales locos, van hasta el río, ahora regresan, no tengas miedo chiquito, y ahí su rostro girando, interrogando, su ansiedad, el temblor de su boca, sus uñas como clavos, y su manos por qué, cómo y su respiración junto a la tuya. Ahora cálmala, tú yo te explico, Toñita, ya se fueron, iban tan rápido, no les vi las caras y ella tenaz, sedienta, averiguando en la negrura, quién, por qué, cómo."[5]

Fuentes affirms here that by disrupting the language the author creates a literary form and structure which grants to each protagonist in the novel a certain intransferable individuality. The author creates a hierarchy of language which serves as the principal vessel through which the content is revealed. Fuentes asserts that Vargas Llosa purposefully disrupts grammatically ("tú pasaron" and "su manos") and syntactically (through the use of commas he reveals the purposeless characteristic of the lives of the protagonists) as he successfully makes the form reflect the predetermined content.

Fuentes further confirms this relationship between form and content in *The Green House* when he says in *La Nueva Novela*...:

> Vargas Llosa no ha esquivado el problema del "contenido" melodramático de unas vidas, que de otra manera, no sabrían su ser. El desamparo, el sentimiento de inexistencia que, en el lenguaje, encuentra sus "outlets" populares en formas tan variadas como el dimunitivo, el circunloquio, el caliche o totacho secreto de las barriadas, la agresión escatológica y porno, en la acción se expresa en la bravuconada, el machismo, la sensiblería, el melodrama (Fuentes, p. 47).

In *The Green House* the content determines the form and the reader cannot separate one from the other without losing elements of reality expressed in the text. In this narrative the seemingly disorganized and disjointed form combines with the omniscient narrative structure and the language to mirror the disorganized, aimless and disrupted life of the characters.

In this chapter Vargas Llosa's *The Green House* has been analyzed utilizing selected concepts of Marxist literary theory. By applying Marx's theory that literature reflects verifiable aspects of historical reality the reader can clearly see that the writer based the novel on empirical historical occurrences in Perú. This makes the novel more credible and authentic. Marx's concept of the relationshp between the economic base and the superstructure permits the reader to grasp the artificial social and economic divisions inflicted on the hierarchichal structure of Iquitos and Piura by the cultivation of rubber and cotton. Finally, Marx's perspective on the relationship between form and content in literature provides another dimension to the novel as it constantly forces the reader to be aware of the devastating effects of monopoly capitalism.

A reading of the novel with these aspects of Marxist literary theory as points of reference provides a better understanding of the sociopolitical content of the narrative.

Chapter 3

A Marxist Reading of
La Muerte de Artemio Cruz

A Marxist reading of Carlos Fuentes's best known novel published in 1962 will make use of several elements of Marxist literary criticism. In particular this analysis emphasizes Fuentes's use of historical events to validate the fictional construction, his emphasis on the critical perspective of society that derives from literature, and his creative and innovative adaptations of narrative form to revolutionary content.

This analysis will utilize, as far as possible, Sam Hileman's English translation, titled *The Death of Artemio Cruz*.[1] The novel is the story of an old revolutionary, Artemio Cruz, related as he lies on his deathbed. As Cruz teeters on the threshold of death, he finds himself surrounded by several people, among them the doctor who attempts to revive him; Catalina, who is trying to comfort him; Father Páez, who is making an effort to give him Extreme Unction and his secretary, Mr. Padilla.

Utilizing a veritable gamut of narrative structures, Fuentes, through Cruz, presents the reader with a panoramic and critical perspective of the historical, social, political and religious evolution of Mexico. The time period that the narrative encompasses is roughly from 1810 up to 1959. As seen through the eyes of Cruz, Mexico appears as a country still in its embryonic evolutionary stage which Fuentes, through Cruz, portrays as being hindered not only by internal corruption at the highest governmental level but also by the apparently negative influence of foreign investments in the country.

The author presents his main protagonist sometimes as a "benevolent dictator" who helps those who have sided with him an have lavished visible and concrete favors on him. At other times

Cruz is pictured as tyrannical and absolutely corrupt, as a man who abuses his power and influence to achieve his less than pure goals. In the end, when Cruz dies a horrible death, the reader finds himself hard-pressed to sympathize with him.

In *The Death of Artemio Cruz* Fuentes paints a depressing picture of stratified corruption in Mexico when he suggests that the idealistic goals of the 1910 Mexican Revolution have been stymied by the destructive personal ambitions of the people and party in power. Fuentes also affirms that the lofty aims of the 1910 Revolution against Porfirio Díaz have been truncated by the disastrous economic effects of foreign and national monopolistic capitalism.

A Marxist reading of this text will begin by a quick re-examination from Chapter 1 of Marx's position on the function of history and reality in a work of art and by an assessment of whether or not this specific principle of Marxist literary theory can be utilized in an analysis of *The Death of Artemio Cruz.*

Art for Marx is a reflection of a particular social reality and portrays its dominant features. However, both Marx and Engels assert that art is not politically prescriptive and that literature does not offer solutions for the political or social conflicts it details. They contend that the novel cannot be openly didactic and that literature is anchored on a social reality which is based on truthful and verifiable historical occurrences. Let us examine the novel with this brief synthesis in mind.

A relevant starting point is a description of what Fuentes himself has said about the role and function of the writer in Latin America. He says:

I do believe very deeply in historical specificity. A writer lives in a given society, and he responds to this society. Now, in the case of Latin America his responsibility is clear. In other more socially and culturally developed countries it is possible that the writer may devote himself strictly to his creative work. In our countries, however, this is very difficult. The creative writer feels an obligation, a responsibility to wield a double sword: the literary and the political. He feels he has to give voice to the voiceless. Our countries generally do not have labor unions; the voiceless do not have political parties. The situation of the newspapers in Latin America, as you know, is deplorable. They are rightist newspapers controlled by foreign influences, by mercantile influences. They do not give a voice to the people, so the creative writer in Latin America feels the urge and responsibility to speak not only for himself as a creative writer, but for the millions who do not have a voice in his country.[2]

By contending that historical specificity is paramount in a work of art in Latin America, Fuentes affirms that the work of art, in this case the novel, has as its basis a historical reality which forms an integral part of a nation's evolutionary stage. If, as he says, the writer responds to the society in which he lives, then it is apparent that this writer portrays in his work realistic aspects of this society. He embodies in this portrayal historical occurrences which complement the epoch and milieu and which correspond to the period in which the work of art is set.

Carlos Fuentes again emphasizes the important role that the depiction of historical reality plays in a novel when he reiterates what the role of the Latin American writer is. He states:

> [In countries]...Bereft of democratic channels of communication, lacking a free press, a responsible Congress, independent labor unions [...] The individual novelist was compelled to be, at once, legislator and reporter, revolutionist and thinker....[He is maintaining]...a continuity of relationship between social manifestation and literary imagination...[He] played the role of redeemer, extended a helping hand to the oppressed Indian, the exploited peasant. That's the attitude at the root of all Latin-American literature. It was a literature of protest in which the writer supplied all the means of communication that were missing in Latin America.[3]

Fuentes considers that one of the functions of the novelist in Latin America is that of analyzing and criticizing values which are representative of the period about which he is writing. He argues:

> La novela actual es una respuesta a la sociedad actual. Más varida, más abundante en expresiones singulares de humanidad, más nutrida de lenguaje poético; menos generalizante, aunque más crítica y más independiente. Esta novela promete ser tan rica, temáticamente, como el país mismo.[4]

If, as Fuentes says, the novel is a reaction against the existing values in a society, then it must credibly portray these values by describing them in the light of the social praxis in which they are anchored. According to Marx, this social praxis must be solidified on real and verifiable historical situations and events. Let us then observe to what extent *The Death of Artemio Cruz* is based on historical reality.

Speaking about the Latin-American novel in general, Fuentes says that it was "born as a form of opposition, of rebellion on the part of the writer, on the part of life itself, as expressed by the writer, against the rigidity of social patterns....The novel arose as a revolt against established order" (Harss and Dohmann, pp.306-307). We logically assume that the "established order" it rebels against was not, in the novelist's eye, a just one. In *The Death of Artemio Cruz* the "established order" against which the novelist rebels has to be an historically empirical one for it to be credible; this, then, is the historical reality that Marx asserted a work of art is based on. In the following paragraphs selected aspects of the Mexican historical reality which Fuentes utilizes to provide credibility to *The Death of Artemio Cruz* will be examined to demonstrate that the novel is anchored in this specific trait of Marxist literary theory. The clearly outlined events and empirically verifiable historical personalities depicted in the text situate the fictional protagonists in the novel within a plausible historical framework. Fuentes relies on historical events (not necessarily in chronological sequence) to portray his fictitious characters as authentic and as functioning from an ambience that is real and historically verifiable.

The narrator utilizes a mixture of fact, that is, historical reality, and fiction, to provide the reader with a believeable text. However, Fuentes is aware that mere linear documentation of historical facts is normally not overwhelmingly interesting. Thus in *The Death of Artemio Cruz* he avoids arbitrary historical narration through the presentation of a multitude of different literary recourses. One of these recourses is the description of a mythical figure (Cruz) in conjunction with historically verifiable events and an innovative narrative technique. Needless to say, these narrative technique demands a conscientious and alert reader [Cortázar's "lector cúmplice" comes to mind].

Fuentes employs fiction to provide new insights into past historical events and to allow the reader to reinterpret history. This reinterpretation of historical facts coerces the reader to become more aware of the importance of the past in shaping the present. Because of his utilization of verifiable historical data, Fuentes implies that the past is pivotal in determining and shaping present and future events. For this writer it is evident that the mixture of historical reality and fictional elements that Fuentes employs bears out the Marxist literary concept that socially valid works of art are situated in a historical reality.

Let us analyze some important aspects of Mexican historical reality that Fuentes uses in *The Death of Artemio Cruz*.

In the novel Fuentes recreates the history of modern Mexico. His "history" spans the era of Santa Anna (approximately) up to the late 1950's. The author freely uses facts, events and people from history and mixes these different elements with mythology. Luis Manuel Villar provides us with some of the historical and social events that Fuentes relies on in this novel. According to him, the following is a chronological synthesis of the historical names and events alluded to or directly mentioned in *The Death of Artemio Cruz*.

1520 Migración de Baracoa (Cuba) a Vera Cruz
1776 Revolución Norteamericana
1810 Grito de Dolores: José María Morelos
1822-1823 El imperio Mexicano: Agustín de Iturbide
1829 Expedición de Barradas
1836 Batalla de San Jacinto: El Alamo
1838 Guerra de los Pasteles
1841-44 Santanismo: Antonio López de Santa Anna
1846-47 y Juan Nepomuceno Almonte
1853-1855
1847 Invasión Norteamericana
1858-61 Guerra de Reforma: Benito Juárez
1864-67 Intervención francesa; Napoleón 111;
 Maximiliano de Habsburgo; Alfonso Dubois de Saligny
1876-80 y Porfiriato: Porfirio Díaz
1884-1911
1910 Deportación de los Indios Yaquis de Sonora a Yucatán
1910-1917 Revolución Mexicana: Lucio Blanco,
Francisco (Pancho) Villa, General Jiménez, Pascual Orozco, Emiliano Zapata
1911-1913 Modernismo: Francisco Madero, Rafael Buelna, Lucio Blanco
1913 Asesinato de Madero por simpatizantes de Victoriano Huerta.
1913-14 Huertismo: Victoriano Huerta

1914-20 Carrancismo: Venustiano Carranza, Pablo González
1920-24 Obregonismo: Alvaro Obregón
1927 Rebelión Cristera e intento de asesinar a Alvaro Obregón:
Miguel Agustín Pro
1930-61 Trujillato: Rafael Leonidas Trujillo
(República Dominicana)
1934-40 Cardenismo: Lázaro Cárdenas
1936 Creación de la CTM (Confederación de
Trabajadores Mexicanos) bajo Vicente
Lombardo Toledano
1936-39 Guerra Civil Española: José Asencio,
Francisco Franco, Federico García Lorca, Enrique Lister, Valentín
González (el campesino), Francisco Galán, Comandante Carlos
1939-45 Segunda Guerra Mundial: Montgomery at El Alamein,
Erwin Rommel
1946-52 Alemanismo: Miguel Alemán
1959 Huelga de ferrocarrileros mexicanos dirigida por Demetrio
Vallejo.
1959-60 Revolución Cubana:Fulgencio Batista.[5]

A quick appraisal of the above chart of historical events
demonstrates clearly the writer's manipulation and utilization of
documented historical occurrences in *The Death of Artemio Cruz.*
The presence of this historical reality serves as a credible backdrop
for the portrayal of fictional events and for the creation of a realistic
character, Artemio Cruz. Fuentes juxtaposes historical reality with
imaginative fiction. This technique of intercalating fact with fiction
adds credibility to the novel; more important, it substantiates the
Marxist literary theory that the work of art is concretized on
verifiable and real historical data. Fuentes mixes empirical historical
events with the fictitious world of a mythical character, Artemio
Cruz. This blending of mythology and reality provides a credible
social praxis for the novel and buttresses the Marxist literary
criterion that a work of art is embedded in proven historical events.
It needs to be emphasized here that although the above chart is in
chronological order, this is not the order in which these events and
historical information are presented in the novel.

The economic situation and the injustices committed by the
Porfirio Díaz regime are also well documented in the novel and
serve as a realistic ambience through which Cruz moves. One of

these historical and economical realities is the description, in the novel, of the general condition of the workers in Mexico prior to the 1910 Revolution. Authentic conflicts between the laborers and the "bosses" which occurred in Cananea in 1906 and in Río Blanco in 1907 are alluded to in the novel. In these two regions of Mexico workers who had attempted to protest labor conditions during the Díaz epoch were attacked by the military and brutally disbanded.

Another example of the portrayal of realistic historical events in the novel occurs with the description of the cruel treatment given to the Yaqui Indians by the military. In the following passage from the novel we are brutally told why the Yaquis were persecuted and how they were killed:

> "Leave them hanging!" shouted Lieutenant Aparicio. He wheeled his horse and with his quirt pushed aside imploring hands. "Let everyone see and remember! So you'll know the kind of men we fight against, men who kill their brothers. Look well! This is how they murdered the whole Yaqui tribe, because the Yaquis wanted to hold on to their land. This is how they murdered the workers at Río Blanco and Cananea, because hunger made them resist. And this is how they'll kill all of you if we don't beat hell out of them! Look, people, look." (p. 74)

The historical and economical mistreatment of the Yaqui Indians by the Díaz regime is utilized here to highlight aspects of the life of the fictitious Cruz. These Indians were mistreated in Mexico because they refused to cede their land to the cronies of Porfirio Díaz. Their mistreatment was one of the major factors that precipitated the 1910 Revolution against Díaz. Again the novelist employs a historical event to provide an authentic environment for the fictitious Cruz.

Yet another example of the utilization of reality in the text is seen through the description of the Labor Unions in post-Revolution Mexico. As we know from history, one of the goals of the Mexican Revolution of 1910 was the formation of Labor Unions. Among other things, these unions were to set standards for minimum wages as well as for fair working hours and amenable working conditions for the laborers. The novelist depicts the betrayal of these goals by the Mexican elite as exemplified by Cruz.

An example of this betrayal in the narrative is Cruz's unfair treatment of the post-1910 Labor Unions in 1958-59, when the Union of Railroad Workers in Mexico went on strike against the Railroad Companies. This strike was a protest by the workers against the social injustices fomented against them by the railroad companies. It was violently suppressed by the bourgeoisie, represented by Cruz, who interpreted it as a communist action and as a threat to Mexican democracy. The fictitious Artemio Cruz uses his power to help quell an event taken by the author from the pages of Mexican history. Since Cruz's extensive holdings included a newspaper, (*Vida Mexicana*), he printed therein articles in support of the wealthy class and deliberately disseminated the erroneous idea that these workers were communists and had to be suppressed. Cruz also played on the public's fear of God and communism to stir opposition to the railroad workers' strike. He says:

> How do you see the situation, Pons?
> Ugly, but easy to take care of, for the moment.
> Well, now we push it in the paper. Hit 'em hard. Don't hold anything back.
> Whatever you say, Don Artemio.
> It's better if we get the public ready.
> We've been plugging at it for so many years.
> I want to see page one and all the editorials. Get me at home, no matter what time.
> Everything will be coordinated. Unmask the red plot.
> Foreign infiltration perverting the essentials of the Mexican Revolution.
> That good old Mexican Revolution!
> Labor leaders manipulated by foreign agents. Tambroni comes out hard. Blanco gives us a pretty column identifying the union head with Antichrist. Blistering cartoons...(p. 53)

Another example of historical reality in the novel occurs in the description of the Agrarian Reform. Designed to help the Mexican peasant better his economic situation, the Agrarian Reform was used by the wealthy landowners to obtain more property and to increase their wealth and influence. Artemio Cruz epitomizes the corruption engendered by this Reform and practiced subsequently by the wealthy class in Mexico. He explains this to Don Gamaliel Bernal:

"You have said it yourself, Don Gamaliel," said the stranger when he returned the next day."You cannot stop events. Let's go on and give up those fields to the peasants. After all, it is land that can only be dry-farmed. You will lose very little. We give it up, so that the Indians will go on raising only patch-crops. And you will see that when they are obligated to us, they'll leave their patches to be hoed by their women, and return to working our irrigated fields for wages. Look: you pass for a hero of the agrarian reform, and it costs you nothing."
(p. 49)

Fuentes, through the fictitious Cruz, describes an actual agricultural program and utilizes it to demonstrate the corruption of his protagonist. Through these examples we can grasp the use of the Marxist literary trait of utilizing historical reality as a backdrop for the realistic portrayal of a character in a work of art. Fuentes again juxtaposes aspects of historical reality with the activities of a fictional protagonist to create a credible personality out of a mythical character. Employing this reality-fantasy combination, the novelist creates in *The Death of Artemio Cruz* a credible "flesh and blood" personality (Artemio Cruz) whom he uses to analyze and criticize past events in the history of Mexico. By using concrete historical events as the environment in which Cruz functions, the writer asserts that the past influences the present and that events that led to the Mexican Revolution of 1810 can re-occur if meaningful social and political reforms are not instituted in Mexico.

In addition to the examples listed above, Fuentes, according to Villar, uses major historical personalities to symbolize major historical events. For example, Villar states that García Lorca represents the Spanish Civil War, Rommel and Montgomery stand for the Second World War and Batista is symptomatic of the Cuban revolution. This combination of empirical historical events with the fictitious development of the protagonist (Artemio Cruz) again substantiates the Marxist view that literature is based on aspects of historical reality. As Villar says about this combination of myth and reality:

Este modo de construcción muestra y plasma las más significativas transformaciones históricas con cierto carácter de darwinismo político: el más fuerte controla el destino político del hombre y de los pueblos. De este modo la novela expone una realidad histórica y a la vez humana, más a su vez plasma la historia como una serie de inevitables crisis en el suceder dialéctico del hombre.

En tanto, Fuentes, al plasmar en la ficción la historia de México, capta las etapas del proceso histórico mexicano hasta llegar a un presente (1961), e nel cual se examinan las causas históricas y sociales para el control de la economía por la burguesía nacional y la lucha de los movimientos populares-sindicatos-en persecución de justicia económica. Así, Fuentes expone la decepción del pueblo por el fracaso de una revolución que sirvió no a los intereses de la masa oprimida sino a los intereses de los revolucionarios burgueses.

Al presentar la historia desde la llegada del europeo a México y su evolución muestra que la problemática social de la década de los 6O tiene su prehistoria de la cual hay que comprender sus etapas para poder comprender los males del presente histórico. Además, en *La Muerte de Artemio Cruz*, se plasma al hombre en el proceso histórico; y juzgando por las grandes lecciones de la historia predice el posible suceder histórico de México.

Por tanto, el marco histórico real ayuda a crear una imagen de la sociedad mexicana genuina que subraya los elementos fundamentales del problema social mexicano de fines del '5O y principios del '6O.Por el profundo contenido histórico-político de la obra, se dice lo que no puede decirse de otra manera: se noveliza una palpable realidad humana. (Villar, pp.294-296).

Through Villar the reader can observe Fuentes's assertion that the great Mexican Revolution primarily served the interests of the wealthy. The profound historical and political content of the novel emphasizes the lessons that are to be learned from history and serves as a credible literary tool to humanize the fictitious Artemio Cruz.

To summarize, we can see that Fuentes weaves verifiable historical accomplishments taken out of the pages of Mexican history into the life of a fictional character whom he names Artemio Cruz; in this manner he uses literary fiction to analyze the history of Mexico and to show the influence of the past on the present. This combination of fact and fiction helps the reader to better comprehend important aspects of Mexican history while at the same time satisfies him esthetically as it makes fiction more authentic.

A second aspect of Marxist literary theory that will be employed in analyzing *The Death of Artemio Cruz* is Marx's assertion that art is a product of the society and this specific society's history. For Marx, art reflects society's evolution, is critical of it and cannot be separated from social praxis. As Epifanio San Juan Jr. says:

> If art is conceived not as an inert product for contemplation but as a mode of interpreting and changing reality, then the real motive force of the imagination exists not in the sphere of noumenal freedom but in the actual tension of class struggle.[6]

This Marxist interpretation of the function of art underscores what was explained as being the function of art in Chapter 1. In the following examples we shall see how Fuentes further depicts reality by providing, through Cruz, a critical view of Mexican society.

At the beginning of the narrative Cruz takes stock of the extent of his wealth and provides the reader with an inkling of the means he employed to accumulate such extensive properties. He says:

> One whole wall of your office is covered by the map that shows the sweep and inter-relationships of your business network: the newspaper in Mexico City, and the real estate there and in Puebla, Guadalajara, Monterrey, Culiacán, Hermosillo, Guaymas, and Acapulco. The sulfur domes in Jaltipán, the mines in Hidalgo, the timber concessions in Tarahumara. The chain of hotels, the pipe foundry, the fish business. The financing operations, the stock holdings, the administration of the company found to lend money to the railroad, the legal representation of North American firms, the directorships of banking houses, the foreign stocks--dyes, steel, and detergents; and one little item that does not appear on the wall: fifteen million dollars deposited in banks in Zurich, London, and New York. Yes: you will light a cigarette, in spite of the warnings you have had from your doctor, and to Padilla will relate again the steps by which you gained your wealth: loans at short terms and high interest to peasants in Puebla, just after the revolution; the acquisition of land around the city of Puebla, whose growth you foresaw; acres for subdivision in Mexico City, thanks to the friendly intervention of each succeeding president; the daily newspaper; the purchase of mining stock; the formation of Mexican-U.S. enterprises in which you participated as front man so that the law would be complied with; trusted friend of North American investors, intermediary between New York and Chicago and the government of Mexico; the manipulation of stock prices to move them to your advantage, buying and selling, always at a profit; the gilded El Dorado years of President Alemán, and your final consolidation; the acquisition of

ejido farm lands taken from their peasant occupants to project new
subdivisions in cities of the interior; the timber concessions. (pp.
1O-11)

Using Cruz as a medium, the novelist paints an unpleasant
picture of the methods employed by the post-Revolution elite to
accumulate wealth. Fuentes projects a critical analysis of this wealthy
class as represented by Cruz, and demonstrates how this bourgeoisie
has betrayed the goals of the Revolution. He documents a realistic
social praxis which delineates not only the corrupt practices of the
wealthy land-owning class (exemplified by Artemio) but also the
unhealthy business connection that exists between these Mexican
capitalists and the capitalists of the United States.
Through Cruz, the author discloses that the landowners added to
their property by "acquiring" lands from the peasants through grants
from succeeding presidents whom thy had helped put to power.
Through the ilegal manipulations of Cruz, the reader acquires a
clear picture of the corrupt nature of the Mexican landowners and
an inkling of some of the dishonest business practices of a representative class of contemporary Mexican society.
Another example of a critical perspective of a social reality
portrayed in *The Death of Artemio Cruz* can be seen in the
following excerpt taken from the novel. In this passage the
conspiracy that exists between foreign (in this case American) and
Mexican capitalists will be perceived.

The North American spread the map on the desk as he removed his
elbows, and the other explained that the zone was so rich that it
could be exploited to the limit until well into the twenty-first century,
to the limit, he repeated, until the deposits ran dry [...] He (Cruz)
demanded two million dollars immediately. They questioned him: to
what account? For although they would cheerfully admit him as their
Mexican partner for an investment of only three hundred thousand,
he had to understand that no one could collect a cent until the domes
began to produce [...] He (Cruz) repeated quietly, those are my
conditions, and let them not suppose that they would be paying him
an advance or anything of that sort: it would merely be what they
owed him for trying to gain the concession for them, and indeed,
without that payment, there would be no concession: in time they
would make back the present they were going to give him now, but
without him, without their front man, their figure-head--and he

begged them to excuse his frank choice of words--they would not be able to obtain the concession and exploit the domes. (p. 2O)

Fuentes, through Cruz, analyzes and criticizes the unfair business practices of the wealthy in Mexican society. Subsequent paragraphs from the novel demonstrate that Artemio's secretary gave the North Americans a series of numbers (presumably secret bank account numbers) into which they were to deposit the bribe money.

Fuentes illustrates a social and political reality that is common in Mexico: Before international or even national businesses can operate, they have to negotiate bribe payments to the appropriate ministers of government.

A third example of the social reality portrayed in *The Death of Artemio Cruz* will further substantiate this specific aspect ofMarxist literary theory.Cruz says:

> This Juan Felipe Couto, as usual wants to be known as sharp [...] He wants to be known as a wheeling and dealing operator like Federico Robles, you remember him. But I am not going to let him push me...[...] It was with my help that he got that highway contract in Sonora. I was able to arrange to have his bid approved when it was a good three times more than the job could possibly cost, for I knew that the highway would pass through some irrigated districts I picked up from ejido farmers. Now I have just found out that the shrewd bastard has bought land himself in that area and is planning to detour the highway so that it will go through his property, not mine...
> Why, but what a swine! And he seems so nice.
> So there you have it, little doll. Now I want you to write a few little rumours in your column, just hinting at our friend's imminent divorce. Very smooth, nothing crude, just enough to let him understand that we mean business. (p. 81)

This form of blackmail is mentioned numerous times in the novel and to a great degree explains one of the methods employed by Cruz to obtain financial independence. In the paragraph that follows this quote in the novel María Luisa says that she has photographs of Felipe in a cabaret with a woman who is not his wife and suggests that this can be published to further slander Couto. Cruz answers that these pictures can be used if Felipe plays stubborn and decides not to bow to his wishes.

The writer, through Cruz, details some of the more corrupt political and social practices of the ruling elite of Mexico. As Marx specified, the work of art reflects realistic aspects of the society it describes. As it portrays these aspects, Marx said, the reader will be made aware of the general ambience in which the work of art is set; by understanding this environment, the conscientious reader will make realistic evaluations and think of positive solutions to the social and political phnomena presented in the work of art. This is what Fuentes achieves in this novel. He couches social and political reality in fiction and myth. However, as Marx specifies, he is not didactic: it is up to the reader to become involved in what the writer says and to react to the injustices and unfair business practices promulgated by the corrupt elite and accurately presented in the novel. In this manner Fuentes presents the involved reader with an aspect of Mexican society and politics that is real and that betrayed one of the goals of the 1910 Mexican Revolution. As Villar says:

> El texto novelístico resulta concretamente en un parcial en juiciamiento de la realidad mexicana, en un estudio crítico del proceso evolutivo de la economía política nacional, en un examen de las fuerzas integrantes en ladialéctica histórica del movimiento obrero de 1958-1959; y, las manipulaciones de la burguesía financiera personificadas en Artemio Cruz para obstruir el proceso social del obrero nacional. Así como encarna la paradoja en que se encuentra México ante una situación de un sistema revolucionario; es decir, por un partido que se nombra retóricamente "revolucionario," pero que somete violentamente el mismo espíritu revolucionario de la masa trabajadora (Villar, pp. 334-335)

Villar suggests that Artemio Cruz represents the financial elite who sprung up after the Revolution and who intentionally hinder the social progress of the national worker. Fuentes in *The Death of Artemio Cruz*, skillfully blends verifiable historical occurrences with fictitious and mythological characters to explain how the lofty goals of the Mexican Revolution were betrayed by greedy and self-centered foreign and national businessmen.

A third characteristic of Marxist literary theory that will be used in this analysis of *The Death of Artemio Cruz* is the relationship that exists between form and content in a work of art. It must be emphasized here that it would be erroneous to classify *The Death of Artemio Cruz* or any other novel as Marxist simply because it may demonstrate some kind of proportional relationship between content and form. In this analysis it will be seen how Marx's theory on the relationship between form and content helps the reader better to grasp the sociopolitical content of the novel.

From Chapter 1 we know that for Marx and Engels form is the product of content and is determined by it. Since content reflects a historical and social evolution, then Marx affirms that it is more subject to change than form. Content therefore has primacy over form and a specific content is articulated in a correspondingly specific form.

The novel shows how the betrayal of the goals of the 1910 Revolution leads to the chaotic social, political and economic status of contemporary Mexico. The writer affirms that the Revolution created a landed oligarchy (represented by Cruz) which is corrupt and which commits different kinds of criminal atrocities to enrich itself and to retain its social position. As a result of this corruption, the protagonists (including Cruz), are presented as psychologically disoriented and as parasitically thriving on the misfortunes of others to better themselves socially and economically. Since in the novel the corruption occurs at the highest government level and since it involves foreign elements, Fuentes strongly suggests in the text that another Revolution is needed in Mexico before the total sociopolitical and economical phenomena become more egalitarian. A description of the socioeconomic environment during the regime of Porfirio Díaz reveals that conditions in Mexico have not been alleviated by the 1910 Revolution. If anything, the novel shows that the economic, social and political elements in Mexico are worse now than before the Revolution.

To mirror this content, Fuentes first inverts chronological time as depicted in the traditional novel. A closer look at this distortion of linear time will show how the form was adapted to reflect the pre-conceived content. Contrary to what happens in normal life, our first encounter with Cruz occurs as he is dying and our last glimpse of him happens at his birth. This inversion of ordinary time sequence is symptomatic of the author's perception of the "death" of Mexico after the 1910 Revolution and of its eventual "birth" after it has been purged of its present corrupt capitalist influence. Cruz, and by extension the corrupt post-Revolution Mexican oligarchy, has literally to die before a new Mexico can be born. This reversal of linear time clearly reflects the content and supports Marx's theory that the form is dependent on it. Fuentes himself has said: "Mexico needs a new revolution. Cubans have brought revolutions up to date."[7] Thus the novelist himself perceives Mexico as a country that needs another revolution to foment the idea of justice and equality; Through the distortion of traditional time we perceive that the message dictates the medium and that the content utilizes this particular reversal of chronological time as the form to express itself more effectively.

A second effect that the distortion of chronological time produces in the novel is suggested by Klaus Meyer-Minnemann. He says that the perception of time practiced by the pre-hispanic civilizations clashes with the perception of time central to the belief of Western society. He suggests that whereas the prehispanic civilizations thought of time as cyclical, the Western society's notion of time hinges on the concept that it is irrevocable and that it produces evolutionary social changes. These changes have served as points of orientation for the different changes in the political system. In the novel Fuentes fuses both perceptions of time as symbolic of the blend of both cultures and as a literary technique to reinforce his belief that post-revolutionary Mexico, with its Western perception of time, has to blend with the old Mexico to produce a more egalitarian society. As Minnemann says:

> La representación de la historia del México moderno en *La Muerte de Artemio Cruz* incluye también la idea del cambio social. Sin embargo, relaciona esta con la concepción prehispánica del tiempo como sucesión de ciclos que le da a la representación de la historia mexicana en la novela un significado especial. El penúltimo episodio antes de la muerte de Artemio Cruz es la noche de San Silvestre de 1955. Le sigue la partida de Artemio de la hacienda de Cocuyo con fecha de 18 de enero de 1903. Al final de la novela coinciden la muerte y el nacimiento del protagonista.[8]

In *Cruz* Fuentes employs a blend of the concepts of time practiced by both civilizations. We visualize Artemio going "backwards in time" to end finally in his birth. By the same token, the author wants us to perceive Mexico as going backwards in time, as purging itself of the existing unfair social and political practices to be born again finally as a nation free of corruption and social and political injustices. The reverse chronology of the novel is a technique whereby the content stimulates the form to enable the reader to understand it more clearly.

The author also uses a specific narrative technique as a device to again demonstrate how the content determines the form. This narrative structure has been analyzed by many literary critics, among whom are: Bienvenido de la Fuente,[9] Gerald W.Petersen,[10] Ileana Araujo[11] and Ethel Hammerly[12] Since their ideas sometimes overlap, in the following paragraphs I will outline some of their reflections on the narrative structure of *Cruz*.

The novel begins with the first person, the "I" form, and in this way the writer initiates the different narrative variations which alternate from the "I" to the "You" and to the "He". "The above-mentioned critics, in particular de la Fuente, suggest that the "I" narrative form represents the present and the conscience of Cruz; the "You" represents the future and the subconscious of the protagonist; and the "He" narrative technique represents the memory of Artemio and the past life of the protagonist. As we can see at the end of the novel, the three narrative forms fuse into one and the three of them die as a symbolic representation of the death of the old Mexico as a prerequisite for the birth of the new Mexico.

The reader perceives Artemio Cruz from the three different angles, and in Cruz he sees the country of Mexico also from three different perspectives. In Cruz the readers see past and present Mexico and the narrative technique enables us to visualize Artemio as the product of the society in which he lived. The "I" narrative structure uses the present tense and permits the reader to achieve a psychological glimpse of the bedridden Cruz, and through him, a clear comprehension of the psychological and physiological makeup of the contemporary Mexican oligarchical structure. As with the inversion of the chronological time sequence, the narrative technique was formulated and adapted to mimic an already conceived content.

The use of the second person (You) and of the future tense suggests that the destiny of Cruz and of Mexico is irrevocable and unavoidable since the destiny of both is predetermined by past historical conditions which cannot be changed. This narrative form embodies part of the content: that is that present day social conditions in Mexico are rooted in the past and are a product of it. Through Cruz, the author tells us that this past historical accomplishments have to be understood before present day social and political conditions can be comprehended.

The third person narrative technique (He) is the most common in the novel and represents the past life of Cruz and correspondingly, of the country of Mexico. This narration in the third person utilizes time in the past and goes back as far as 1899 to present an objective account of Cruz's and Mexico's history. In reality, this third person relates all of Cruz's life and, through him, we again observe the historical events which have shaped his life and, by extension, the contemporary social and political life of the country. The "He" narrative technique depicts works of Cruz and presents him as the product of the environment in which he lived.

To summarize, the critics mentioned above assert that the narration in the first person provides the reader with an insight into the psychological character of the oligarchical elite in Mexico. The second person narrative technique allows us to see the effects of the past on present day Mexican society. The deeply historical third person narrative form presents Cruz as being a product of his ambience and as the previously mentioned critics affirm, is the voice of the omniscient author.

With this tri-vocal narrative form the author examines the entire life of Cruz and of Mexico. This innovative method of description enables the reader to perceive the country and people of Mexico both as a blend and as a product of past historical events. In this way the novelist uses the narrative form to mirror the all-important content. By mixing the historical with the mythical and articulating this historical content in an innovative form, the novelist provides the reader with factual data of the history of Mexico.

A careful reading of the text shows that the three-person narrative technique corresponds perfectly with the chaotic mental state of Cruz. Petersen suggests that this correspondence between content and form is especially perceived at the end of the novel when the three "personalities" of Cruz blend into one and they all die. As Cruz himself says at the very end of the text:

> "Artemio Cruz...Name...hopeless...heart message...hopeless...You will not know. I carry you inside and with you I die. The three, we...will die. You...die, have died...I will die." (p. 306)

The real death of Cruz symbolizes the fictional death of the country, a death of purification which will cleanse Mexico of the priviledged oligarchy and usher in a more just and equal society.

Finally, the "I" "You" and "He" narrative technique (form) used by Fuentes helps the alert reader gain a more comprehensive view of the content and demonstrates the effectiveness of this Marxist literary concept in helping us better to analyze and comprehend *The Death of Artemio Cruz*. The use of this type of narration to formulate the preconceived content permits the novelist to situate the protagonist within the socio-economic,cultural and historioical framework that existed in Mexico during the time period that the text encompasses. This narrative technique makes us visualize Cruz as a product of his environment, powerless to fight his destiny, which has been dictated by history.

As a product of his surroundings, Cruz represents the failure of the ideals of the Mexican Revolution and symbolizes the rise of a new privileged and elitist class after the Revolution. As Don Gamaliel says in the novel: "Unfortunate land...unfortunate land where each generation must destroy its masters and replace them with new masters equally ambitious and rapacious." (p. 45) This three-pronged narrative form is an indispensable literary tool in analyzing the novel. As Bienvenido de la Fuente says:

Las secuencias narradas en primera persona nos presentan en un primer plano los momentos de agonía de Artemio Cruz. Por medio de monólogos interiores van siendo revelados, junto a las sensaciones dolorosas que siente en estos momentos el moribundo, ciertos episodios de su vida, que le vienen a la mente y que le desasosiegan tanto como los dolores físicos. En las secuencias narradas en tercera persona un narrador omnisciente da noticia de 12 momentos iniciales de la vida de Artemio Cruz. Estos episodios están fijados en el tiempo y en el lugar, pero son narrados no cronológicamente, sinoconforme van viniendo a la memoria del protagonista en los delirios de sus últimas horas de vida.
[...] En las secuencias narradas en primera persona se hallan ya como en gérmen prácticamente todos los puntos centrales de la novela, si bien nos son narrados de tal forma, que la mayor parte de ellos sólo nos son inteligibles en una segunda lectura (De la Fuente,pp.144-145)

Artemio remembers events disjointedly,and Fuentes expresses these reminiscences in a non-chronologicalmanner, mimicking the way in which they are remembered. This technique of narration enables the reader to better understand the confused and chaotic social and economic state of Mexico as represented by the equally confused and chaotic mental state of Cruz.

A third example from the novel which demonstrates the predominance of the content over the form can be found in the use of the language and in the syntax. Before these two literary elements can be discussed, it is important to remember that the story is narrated from the deathbed of Cruz (something that the reader can easily forget) and that because of this peculiar style of narration, the employment of flashbacks contributes greatly to the general comprehension of the content. This use of flashbacks permits the reader to glimpse episodes in history that have shaped the life of the protagonist and the contemporary social and political environment of Mexico. Within this context the language will be studied as a narrative form that complements the content and that substantiates the Marxist literary theory that the content determines the form.

The importance of language as an effective means of projecting content can not be attributed solely to Marx. One can not therefore categorize *The Death of Artemio Cruz* as Marxist simply because it may employ innovative use of the language to mirror the content. A better understanding of the Marxist use of the language, however, will help us better grasp the content of the novel. One critic of literature who has discussed the function of language in a work of art is Hayden White. He says: "Great works of fiction will usually[...] not only be about their putative subject-matter, but also about language itself and the problematical relation between language consciousness and reality--including the writer's own language" [13].

The language not only describes the content (subject-matter) but also examines itself and helps bridge the gap between awareness of the language itself and reality. Fuentes himself shows his knowledge of the relationship between language and reality when he affirms that the language demonstrates a social reality. He asserts:

> [...] Nuestro verdadero lenguaje [...] está en el proceso de descubrirse y de crearse y, en el acto mismo de su descubrimiento y creación, pone en jaque, revolucionariamente, toda una estructura económica, política y social fundada en un lenguaje verticalmente falso. Escribir sobre América Latina, desde América Latina, para América Latina, ser testigo de América Latina en la acción o en el lenguaje significa y, significará cada vez más, un hecho revolucionario. Nuestras sociedades no quieren testigos. No quieren críticos. Y cada escritor,

como cada revolucionario, es de algún modo eso: un hombre que ve,
escucha, imagina y dice: un hombre que niega que vivimos en el
mejor de los mundos[14]

In *The Death of Artemio Cruz* Fuentes adapts the language to
reflect the mental state of the various characters, in this way
adapting it to express the content. A few examples of this from the
text will illustrate this particular use of the language.

Firstly, the language is utilized to criticize and to ridicule the
mentality of foreign consumption of the priviledged class in Mexico.
Cruz, representing this class in the novel, eats a meal at the Club
consisting of "Vichysoisse, lobster, Côtes du Rhone, and Baked
Alaska." (p. 151) Another example of Cruz's preference for foreign
consumer goods occurs at his home. He orders his servant to bring
him a very dry Martini and to get it the servant slid open the carved
cedar panels of a mirrored niche. Inside the niche there was:

a showcase of colored labels and decantered liquids: opalescent,
emerald, green, red, crystalline: Chartreuse, Peppermint, Acquavit,
Vermouth, Courvoissier, Long John, Calvados, Armagnac, Beherovka,
and Penrod: rows of crystal glasses, thick and stubby, thin and ringing.
(p.244)

Yet another example of the language reflecting the Mexicans'
penchant for foreign consumer goods occurs as Cruz flies from
Sonora to Mexico City. He reclines in his seat and as the plane
enters the Valley of Mexico the NO SMOKING, FASTEN SEAT
BELTS signs appear, all in English but in a Mexican airplane, flying
within the country of Mexico. Fuentes in this manner projects a
powerful criticism of Mexico's dependency on foreign technology. As
Villar says: "El uso estructural de los anglicismos complementa la
actitud psicológica de los personajes hacia la sociedad mexicana y
hacia los Estados Unidos" (Villar, p. 362).
Cruz's bourgeois mentality is expressed in the description of what he
eats and what he drinks. The language expresses both the content
and the mental process that changes as a result of foreign influence
in the economy and in the society. For example, Cruz's outlook on
life changed when he became involved with the North Americans;
now one of his goals was to imitate a foreign way of thinking and to

demonstrate his economic and social superiority through his use of English and of foreign products. As Villar says:

> [...] Desde el punto de vista del lenguaje, la novela es una totalidad de elementos lingüísticos fácilmente descifrados dentro de la sociedad; y, seleccionados a conciencia para establecer una eficaz relación emisor- receptor. De ahí la profunda representación de lo que Fuentes califica en un ensayo posterior como "la palabra enemiga" (Villar, p. 380).

Fuentes adapts the language to mirror the different mental and physical states of the protagonists. For example, Cruz utilizes the language of humility and frustration when he tries to imitate the North Americans. He says:

> You will feel satisfied to have imposed your will upon them-confess it: you imposed your will so that they would admit that you are their equal: seldom have you felt happier. For ever since you began to be what you are, to learn to appreciate the feel of fine cloth, the taste of good liquor, the scent of rich lotions, all those things that in recent years have been your only, isolated pleasures; ever since then you have lived with regret for the geographical error that has prevented you from being one of them. You admire their efficiency, their comforts, their hygiene, their power, their strength of will; and you look around you and find intolerable the incompetence, misery, dirt, the weakness and nakedness of this impoverished country that has nothing. You ache because you know that no matter how hard you try, you can never be what they are but can become at most only a pale copy, a near approximation. (p. 28)

About this specific use of language to embody the content Fuentes says in *La Nueva Novela*...:

> Nuestra literatura es verdaderamente revolucionaria en cuanto le niega al orden establecido el léxico que este quisiera y le pone el lenguaje de la alarma, la renovación, el desorden y el humor. El lenguaje, en suma de la ambiguedad de significados, de la constelación de alusiones: de la apertura (p.32).

Fuentes suggests that one of the reasons why Latin-American literature is revolutionary is that it does not use conventional language; instead the language changes to reflect the disorder and the ambiguity that exist in the reality that the work of art is portraying. Fuentes admits that this need to adapt the language to reflect the environment being described has made the Latin-American writer refocus both his style and his aim in writing. He says:

> El escritor latino americano deja de ser un ente pintoresco y regional para situarse frente a la condición humana [...] Para el escritor mexicano, con el ánimo liberal e independista surgió la imagen estereotipada que desplazaría a la naturaleza: el dictador.De aquí que la literatura se tradujera entonces en denuncia y protesta[15]

Fuentes in this manner suggests that the language has to be adapted to reflect the contemporary reality that surrounds the protagonist at diverse times during his lifetime.

The syntax in the novel is another effective means through which the form is adapted to express the content. Fuentes distorts traditional syntax by juxtaposing paragraphs consisting of one line to paragraphs encompassing many pages. For example, on page 159 of the novel he has Cruz talking in the form of a long interior monologue which spans four pages and is expressed in one paragraph only. This four-page monologue is representative of Cruz's memory, which comes in haphazard bursts and which therefore has to be printed with an almost feverish haste since a dying man can easily forget specific items that he wants to remember. The novelist captures this sense of urgency by allowing no syntactical break in Cruz's interior monologue and through this means allows the form to mirror the content.

Another unconventional adaptation of the syntax occurs with the innovative use of the future tense to describe past events. Early in the novel Cruz says:

> Yes: yesterday you will fly home from Hermosillo. Yesterday, the ninth of April, 1959, you will fly back in the regular flight of the Compañía Mexicana de Aviación, leaving Sonora's capital and it's infernal heat at exactly nine-fifty-five in the morning, arriving in Mexico City at exactly four-thirty in the afternoon.(p. 8)

The future tense, as can be seen, expresses the past and totally distorts regular syntactical rules. According to Joseph Sommers:

> El efecto general del uso del futuro es el de colocar al lector al lado
> de Cruz a medida que vuelve a vivir sus crisis personales, dando la
> impresión de que éstas no han ocurrido todavía y que Cruz aun tiene
> opciones, lo que le permite al lector identificarse con sus problemas
> [16].

The use of the future tense to express past events lets the reader identify with Cruz and creates the illusion that Cruz still has options and that Mexico has the choice of bettering its economic and political situation if it learns from the past.

In *Cruz* Fuentes exposes the corruption that occurred in Mexico after the 1910 Revolution and suggests that the ruling PRI political party betrayed the aims of the Revolution by representing the capitalists instead of the laborers. Through this novel, Fuentes acquaints the reader with the economical, political and social forces that are at work in post-Revolution Mexico. He suggests that these forces are grounded in history and are essential in making contemporary Mexican politics, economics and society what it is. As Fuentes himself says:

> [...] it is frequently said that the flaw of American foreign policy is its
> incapacity to understand the changes that are coming about in the
> underdeveloped world: that flaw can only be corrected through
> knowledge of the people making these changes and of the context of
> their actions[17].

In this novel we can observe that Fuentes wants to acquaint the reader with the various different forces at work in the Mexican society. In this manner the author ensures that the reader will have a better understanding of why Mexico is the way it is and why the people are the way they are.

To conclude, the key facets that are illuminated by an application of three principles of Marxist literary theory in this novel are: the historical panorama of Mexico from 1810 to 1961 which serves to validate the fictional narrative. That is, the author's attention to historical detail enables him to anchor his protagonist in a clearly defined social praxis that readers cannot ignore. Second, Fuentes's novel provides a critical perspective of the society of which it is a product. In this respect *Artemio Cruz* satisfies one of Marx's primary requisites for socially relevant fiction. Third and finally, it has been shown how the form [inverted chronological order, narrative structures and language] of *Artemio Cruz* was shaped by the revolutionary content. *The Death of Artemio Cruz*, like Mexican society, is, as Marx might have said, a window on an evolutionary process involving unending destruction of old forms and creation of new ones.

Chapter 4

A Marxist Reading of Puig's
Boquitas Pintadas

Written in the form of a soap opera, *Heartbreak Tango*[1] describes the life of Juan Carlos Etchepare, a stereotypical Latin-American "macho" for whom the women fight and who in the end dies of tuberculosis. Intertwined with Juan Carlos's life-story is that of the women he loved (Nélida, Mabel, his sister Celina, his mother Leonor, and the widow Elsa). Puig also provides descriptions of Coronel Vallejos the wretched provincial town which serves as the setting for the novel, and of Buenos Aires.

A careful reading of the novel shows that the author exposes the exaggerated emphasis Argentinians (both provincial and cosmopolitan) place on an artificial social "pecking order." This superficial class division prompts one to consider that a Marxist analysis of the text will help the reader better to understand it and to interpret it as a serious comment on the Argentinian social milieu. This same contrived class distinction, as shown in the text, leads to the first concept of Marxist literary theory that will be used to analyze this novel:namely Marx's assertion that the concept of "art for art's sake" is invalid.

Both Marx and Engels affirmed that literature and other esthetic phenomena are produced in a socio-historical context which encompasses the sum total of man's activities. Thus literature for them is based on the social texture of man and man's works, and since man's nature is irrevocably social, then there can exist no such thing as "pure" art, in the sense of art that is not anchored in a social praxis.

The first element in the novel that suggests that the novel is based on societal realities can be seen in Puig's description and criticism of the rigid and artificial class structure in Vallejos. The society in this town (and later in Buenos Aires) is strictly compartmentalized into the "haves and have-nots." The artificial boundaries that prevent an intermixture between people of the various social strata are clearly delineated and seemingly closely respected by members of each social class.

At the top of the social pyramid in Coronel Vallejos is the young and wealthy British rancher, Cecil Borough-Croydon, Mabel's suitor and her parents' favorite. For them and for Mabel his money and social status represent an achieveable and desirable step up the social ladder. Mabel however does not truly love him. For her he represents economic security as well as upward social mobility, and she accepts his courtship for these reasons. In actuality she loves Juan Carlos but is concerned about his disease. In the end Mabel's father, Don Antonio Sáenz, is the victim of a law suit by the same Cecil Borough-Croydon because he had deliberately sold the rancher diseased cattle. Cecil wins the suit and breaks off his engagement to Mabel. She and her family are impoverished by Cecil's successful suit, and since her marriage to Cecil was cancelled, Mabel's chances of climbing the social ladder are curtailed.

Puig intentionally uses an aristocratic-sounding British name for the man at the top of the social hierarchy, who, incidentally, is not even a native. This is the author's way of ridiculing a society which allows for its own division/exploitation by a foreign entity.

Immediately below Cecil Borough-Croydon in the town's social strata are the businessmen and professionals like Antonio Sáenz, Doña Leonor, the retired mother of Juan Carlos who lives on a pension, Celina, a schoolteacher and Juan Carlos's sister and Dr. Nastini, the town's only medical doctor. Ranked with this group are also the government employees like Juan Carlos, who worked in the mayor's office, and Mabel who is also a school teacher. This group represents the second rung in the descending social ladder and the author demonstrates the vicious manner in which they jealously guard their contrived position in society. Puig also highlights their hypocrisy as they struggle financially to afford the physical accoutrements that society generally associates with people of their social caliber.   For example, Antonio Sáenz (Mabel's father), evidently in need of cash to maintain the standard of living his self-designated "position" in society demands, openly encourages the wealthy Borough-Croydon to court his daughter, and tangibly discourages her from seeing Juan Carlos. He invites Cecil for dinners at his home and prompts his daughter to accept Croydon's invitation for a weekend visit to his ranch.

Mabel reluctantly accedes only to be disappointed by Cecil's unemotional declaration of "love" for her. He attributes his unimpassioned courtship to his hereditary British frigidity, the author's way of criticizing this legendary British personality trait. Mabel can not help comparing him, unfavorably, to the amorous and passionate Juan Carlos. Borough-Croydon, as was mentioned, refuses to marry her after the legal incident with her father. This not only truncates Mabel's and her father's chances of climbing up the social ladder but also catapults her into a masochistic love-hate affair with Pancho, a man whom she considers beneath her self-imposed social class, and whom she labels "half-breed" and hates even as he is making love to her.

The above-mentioned Pancho had fathered an illegitimate child with Fanny, Mabel's family's maid. He had refused responsibilty for the child and Fanny murders him one night as he is leaving Mabel's bedroom. Mabel convinces her to lie to the police about her reason for killing Pancho. Fanny childishly tells the police that Pancho had been attempting to sexually molest her and that she had been forced to defend herself. Puig poignantly demonstrates the dishonest manner in which Mabel convinced the maid to lie for her and to take all the blame for Pancho's death when Mabel confessing to the priest says:

> When the police asked me what had happened I got up the nerve God knows how...and I lied to them. I told them the boy tried to take advantage of the maid and that she defended herself with the kitchen knife...No the maid didn't wake up until the next morning, I spent the whole night by her side, and I was so insistent that the doctor didn't let them take her to the police station, and so they left a sergeant on watch who went to the kitchen from time to time to eat...When the poor wretch woke up I told her that if she told the truth they would condemn her to life imprisonment and she would never see her son again. I explained it till she understood that she wasn't to say anything about the boy being in my room, that he had jumped over the wall to see her, to take advantage of her again, and that it was no longer worth the trouble to get back at me, the main thing was to save herself so that she'd be able to give her baby all the comforts-a manner of speech-and I explained very clearly to her

what she had to put in her statement. She looked at me without
saying a word. And everything came out fine. She understood that
she had to lie for them to let her go. And everybody believed it was
in legitimate defense. (p. 190)

The hypocrisy of this social class as represented by Mabel is seen
through her confession, and so she convinced the illiterate maid to
accept all the blame while she herself was exonerated.

But perhaps the greatest hypocrisy exhibited by this social class
represented by Mabel occurs when she later marries without telling
her husband about her previous affair. This constitutes in the
reader's eye another dishonest act, culminated by the final episode
in which we see an unhappy Mabel about to engage in an illicit
extra-marital affair with a neighborhood store clerk, an employee
who she herself would consider quite below her inflated social rank.

Through Mabel, Puig also casts aspersions on the social practice
of matrimony. Through her he implies that society prompts its
members to marry for convenience rather than for love and that
respectful members of society see nothing intrinsically wrong with
this social phenomenon. At the beginning of the narrative Mabel
seeks advice from the Lonelyhearts column of the magazine
Feminine World. She had written to the editor of this column to
explain the dilemma in her love life. According to her letter, she
loved Juan Carlos but her father didn't like him because he was
poor and sick with a contagious disease. She tells the editor that
there is a young rich man of English origin whom her father likes;
she further confesses that this Englishman has invited her to spend
a holiday weekend at his ranch and that her father wants her to
go; Juan Carlos, however, has vowed that he will break up with her
if she goes. She asks the columnist for advice. The columnist
(María Luisa Díaz Pardo) replies:

I don't envy the bewilderment of your soul but rather all that you
have in life. I don't think that you love your admirer (Juan Carlos)
enough to confront a break with your parents. Your case is typical
of young girls brought up in the heart of a happy and prosperous
family. To continue your flirtation (excuse the term) would mean
destroying that family harmony you already feel threatened. And
believe me, for a flirtation one shouldn't pay such a price. You are
very young and can wait for the knight on the white horse who is to

everyone's taste. Have a good time at the ranch, study English, and in case you two have to make signs in order to communicate please don't nod your head yes too often! By using that sign sparingly you will conquer the world and, even more important, you will secure your happiness and that of your parents...(pp. 38-39)

Through Pardo Puig's critical social commentary on the values of and reasons for marriage is clearly made. In the end Mabel marries for convenience's sake (not to Juan Carlos or Cecil) and is on the verge of committing adultery because she obviously is unhappy.

Through Doña Leonor, Puig again shows how literature critically describes the social milieu. Doña Leonor is a widow who lives on a frugal pension left to her by her defunct husband. Celina, her daughter, is a schoolteacher. Although Doña Leonor has problems making "ends meet," she pampers her son Juan Carlos, who works when he wants to and does not contribute towards the financial support of the family. Both Doña Leonor and Celina cater to Juan Carlos's every wish. They refuse to admit that he is a lazy, no-good womanizer, a man who stops at nothing to satisfy his ego and sexual appetite.

Since Doña Leonor does not have a husband she doesn't consider herself as well off as Don Antonio Sáenz and his family. Hence both she and Celina encourage Juan Carlos to court Mabel in the hopes that a marriage between the two can uplift them economically and socially. It is ironic that Juan Carlos is a "Don Juan" while at the same time Celina, his sister, has a reputation for jumping into bed with anyone that comes along. In this manner Puig criticizes the hypocrisy of members of this "middle" class who dare to judge others while they themselves are full of moral flaws. As an example of their pampering of Juan Carlos, Puig describes the following scene between them. Juan Carlos is ill and goes to bed without eating. As the author says:

[...] A few minutes later they took the meal to his bed on a tray. Juan Carlos found that the steak was cold. They took it back to the grill, Celina let it touch the iron on one side and then the other just a few seconds so that it wouldn't cook too much. His mother and Celina were standing in the room looking at him, waiting for some order. Juan Carlos asked them to go finish their lunch... (p. 53)

Puig makes us perceive the selfishness of Juan Carlos and negatively comments on the servility of the women. When Juan Carlos has to leave Vallejos to undergo expensive treatment for his illness, Doña Leonor realizes that she cannot pay for it. One of Juan Carlos's lovers (the widow DiCarlo) decides to sell her house and move to the city where he will receive treatment. She plans to establish a boardinghouse in this town and take care of Juan Carlos herself. Celina and her mother are not in agreement because this will show that they (Doña Leonor's family) have been living under false pretenses. They have no money to effect Juan Carlos' cure in Cosquín; however they don't want anyone to know as this would disgrace them socially. In what is perhaps the strongest criticism of the falseness of this social class Puig explains what Celina did to keep secret the widow's intentions. Celina visits DiCarlo and says: (The italicized sections from the text are omitted).

> -Well, mama, and I too, are asking you for one thing: You won't have any opposition from us, but we ask you not to tell anybody that you are going to Cosquín.
> -Don't worry, I wasn't thinking of telling anybody, and I am not telling my daughter everything either...
> -...Anyway...people are going to realize if you are not more careful. For example the furniture, don't send it from here...Send the furniture to your daughter's in Charlonne, and from there to Cosquín. And take the same precautions for everything.
> -What other precautions?
> Everything. So that nobody finds out you're there with my brother. You have to understand that it's a disgrace to our family.
> -If God sent your brother that illness it was God's will, you don't gain anything by feeling disgraced.
> -But do you promise to do that with the furniture and the deed to the house?...
> -I promise. (pp. 168-169)

Both Celina and her mother are in a precarious financial position, yet their pride won't allow them to accept help and even when they do, they don't want the donor to make it public as this will disgrace them in society's eyes.

Even Nastini, the medical doctor, does not escape Puig's social criticism. He employs Nélida as his medical assistant and, although married, wants to have an affair with her. She gives in, the implication being that she may lose her employment if she resists his advances. The doctor unscrupulously uses her sexually and when his wife finds out, he fires Nélida. Puig implies that the doctor gossiped about his sexual liason with her and the stigma of this relationship haunts the young girl. It adversely affects her relationship with other men since she is afraid that they will find out that she is not a virgin and abandon her. Nastini continues to attempt to seduce his other employes, like Fanny the maid. Although the doctor is economically self-sufficient, like Sáenz he is dishonest since he takes advantage of his social position to seduce his female workers. In this respect Nastini is no better than Juan Carlos, although his position in the social ladder is somewhat higher.

Again the novelist comments on the dishonesty of this social class when he describes the actions and self-serving intentions of Juan Carlos. To Pancho Juan Carlos said the following about Nené:

> Juan Carlos said (to Pancho) that as soon as he got what he was after, there would be no more Nené, and asked Pancho to swear not to tell anyone: Mabel had promised to convince the Englishman to take him on as the manager of both ranches. Juan Carlos added that one owner can't be at two ranches at the same time, and being the manager is like being the owner of one of the two. Pancho asked him if he would continue with Nené in the event that he got that job. Juan Carlos replied that he asked that question because he didn't know anything about women [...] Juan Carlos said that Nené was like all the rest, if one treated her nice she acted up, if one treated her bad she stayed in line. The important thing was to make Mabel jealous so that she wouldn't forget to do him that favor. (p. 68)

Nené is the unfortunate victim of both Juan Carlos and Nastini: They both use her to serve their distinctive purposes; Juan Carlos to make Mabel jealous so that she will provide him with the position as Borough-Croydon's foreman; Nastini to satisfy his sexual appetite. They both dump her once their purposes are served. Nélida's life is ruined as a result of their manipulations and she is forced to accept an unprestigious position as a wrapper in the Argentine Bargain Store, a position which is considerably less in social stature and most likely in pay than that of a doctor's assistant.

In descending order, the other social group in Coronel Vallejos is represented by Nélida and her family. Because of her lowly job at the Argentine Bargain Store she was made to feel socially inferior to Celina and Mabel who, because they were both teachers, thought of themselves as Nélida's social superior. This sense of superiority limited Nélida's social activities as it in effect barred her from participating in events that demanded a monetary fee to guarantee participation. Celina's dislike for Nélida was also fueled by the fact that she wanted her brother to marry Mabel rather than Nené as this would presumably uplift her socially. Puig makes it clear that the social divisions were rigid and that members of one social category were not allowed to overstep the artificially created boundaries that separated them from the members of the other group. Nélida explains this in her letter to Doña Leonor:

It all began at the time I started working as a packer at the Argentine Bargain Store, and because I had been friends since grammar school with Celina and Mabel who were already back in Vallejos with their teaching licenses-Mabel a girl with money besides-I began going to the Social Club.
Now Mrs. Etchepare, I admit that that was the wrong move, and all for not listening to mama. And did she hit the nail on the head that time: she told me not to go to the dances at the club. What girls went to the club? Girls who could dress well, or because their parents had a good position, or because they were teachers, but as you will remember the girls from the stores went to the Recreational Club instead. Mama told me that pushing myself where I didn't belong would only bring trouble. No sooner said than done. That very same year, they were preparing those numbers for the spring festival and they chose me and not Celina. In Mabel's case we knew for sure they'd choose her, because her father cracked the whip at the club [....] In the first rehearsal [....] Celina came over and started talking into my ear instead of letting me concentrate on the music. She said she didn't want to be my friend anymore because they had let me into the club thanks to her and now I didn't join her in protest against them leaving her out in the cold. She had already asked me not to accept, in sympathy, but she didn't ask Mabel the same thing, and that made me angry. Why didn't she dare to say the same thing to Mabel? Because Mabel had money and I didn't? Or because she was a teacher and I hadn't gone further than sixth grade? I don't know why Celina wanted to sacrifice me and not the other one [...] But to finish the thing with Celina, I'm going to be

frank: what she whispered in my ear was that if it hadn't been for her I wouldn't have set foot in the club, and that everybody knew about Doctor Nastini. (pp. 21, 22 and 23)

Nélida's emotional confession succinctly delineates the rigid divisions that existed between each social group in Vallejos. In the eyes of society (as represented by Mabel and Celina) Nélida was an outcast who did not belong in the Social Club, since she worked as a clerk rather than as a teacher. Instead she had to be content with being a member of the Recreational Club, a facility built for members of her social group.

The bottom rung of the social group in Vallejos is represented by Francisco Catalino Páez (Pancho) and by Antonia Josefa Ramírez (Big Fanny). Both of them are common laborers, Pancho a bricklayer and Fanny a maid first for Nastini and then for Doña Leonor. Being very poor, they live at the margin of society. Pancho fathers Fanny's bastard child but refuses to take responsibility for him. Puig describe in detail the environment in which they function. Pancho, for example, lives in a two room shack with his parents, two sisters and a brother. In contrast to Mabel's home, Pancho's has no kitchen or bathroom. A day in Pancho's life follows this pattern:

Pancho woke up at 5:3O as usual, although the day had not yet dawned [...]in the lot behind their shack was a water pump. He wet his face and hair, he rinsed his mouth. He went into the room to put on overalls. His two sisters were sleeping in a big bed, his brother in a corner on a canvas cot. Pancho's bed had springs and a burlap mattress. The shack had a dirt floor, adobe walls, tin roof. His parents slept in the only other room with their youngest son, seven years old. Pancho was the oldest boy [...] He lit the coal in the stove and prepared boiled mate with milk. He looked for bread, couldn't find it. He awakened his mother; at the bottom of a sack of pumpkins two biscuits had been hidden for Pancho. The biscuits were white, made of flour and fat, Pancho's teeth were big and square, but stained, from the salty pump water. His mother told him that he had thick hair like hers, like the Indians, and curly like his Valencian father's. His mother asked him to make a muscle and then felt his arm, her son wasn't very tall but he was strong all right, without knowing why she thought of the bear cubs in a circus that had passed through Vallejos, and handed him another cup of boiled mate. (pp. 64 & 65).

Puig's Zolaesque description of Pancho's habitat and of his physical appearance vigorously highlights the difference in social rank between the haves (like Mabel) and the have-nots. Being of Indian descent, Pancho is considered racially inferior and derrogatorily referred to as "half-breed" by both his "good friend" Juan Carlos and by Mabel. Pancho's social stature is also clearly indicated when he is constantly referred to as the bricklayer rather than as a construction worker. Somehow "bricklayer" connotes inferiority, of someone who is down the scale in the construction-worker hierarchy.

To better his social standing Pancho decides to become a policeman. Although this decision may have improved his social and financial situation, it has the negative effect of encouraging Pancho to deny siring Fanny's son as he imagines that his acceptance of a bastard child may jeopardize his career and his chances of promotion. Ironically, Pancho's position as policeman gives him access to Mabel's home since the police station adjoined Mabel's house. This encourages Pancho to embark on a revengeful sexual affair with Mabel, which in the end leads to his murder by Fanny. Pancho's efforts at bettering his position in society were his own undoing. Pancho's relationship with Mabel may also have been prompted by his desire to better himself socially. He thought of it as a means to humiliate her and as a means to show a member of the "superior" race that he was in control. Pancho describes Mabel's room in the following manner:

[...] The dolls on the shelf, natural hair and eyes that move, if I want I can twist their arms, legs, head, until they hurt because at night dolls can't scream, the three banners, the wooden cross, and the bronze Christ, the picture frame, the bureau, the wardrobe, the perfumed pillow case, my black head on the white pillow, the sheet is embroidered with fake flowers and a frilly fringe links them together from one tip of the bed to the other, the wool blanket cropped off some tame little sheep, she lets the billy goat come near her: the life-sized doll is all covered up, I wake her up when I want to, in the dark her black hair and mouth, the dolls sitting on the shelf, they don't move, I twist them around and turn their heads, their arms, legs, they can't scream because the father will come and

see me: I twist one arm, I twist the other arm, they can't stand the
pain any longer but if they shout they're discovered, the half-breed's
dark skin smudged your embroidered sheets? He smudges your
mouth and ears and your whole body from twelve at night till three,
four in the morning, did he smudge your conscience? Don't you have
any regrets? [...] Where's my undershirt? [...] lazy thing, the doll
sleeps, the natural hair and the eyes that move, wake up, I'm going
now, you have to close the window after I jump.... (pp. 153-154).

This graphic description of Pancho's perception of his sexual
encounter with Mabel underscores his position in society. He wants
to humiliate her and dares her to cry during the sexual act so her
father can hear them and come to her room and see them. For him
this will be a triumph as Don Antonio will realize what the
half-breed is doing to his daughter.

Pancho's illicit involvement with Mabel stems from a sense of
revenge at being made to feel socially inferior (even though he is a
policeman) while Mabel's motives stem from a masochistic desire to
punish herself after losing Cecil, her one chance at upward social
and economic mobility. Puig starkly contrasts Pancho's and Mabel's
"bedroom:" While he sleeps on a burlap-covered mattress with his
brothers, she sleeps in her own bedroom with perfumed pillow cases
and embroidered sheets; the fake flowers of the embroidered sheets
are emblematic of the falseness of Pancho's "new" social status
acquired because he is now a policeman. These fake flowers are also
symbolic of the superficial and fraudulent nature of Pancho and
Mabel's relationship: he is motivated by a desire for revenge and a
desire to show his domination of a supposedley superior being; she
participates because of an instinct for self-flagellation because she
feels she deserves punishment after failing to keep Cecil.

Big Fanny is the other representative of this bottom social rung
in Vallejos. She is at first a maid for Nastini, lives in his house and
sleeps in a bedroom similar to Pancho's. Puig describes this
bedroom in the following manner:

[...] The first thing she saw was the heap of objects stored in her
room: bottles of bleach, jugs of wine, cans of oil, a cask of port wine,
strings of garlic hanging from the wall, sacks of potatoes, onions,
cans of kerosene, and bars of soap. Her bedroom was also a pantry.
Instead of a bathroom she had to make do with an old outhouse and

the laundry sink, at the rear of the courtyard. There, at 6:35, she washed her face, neck, and armpits...(p. 70)

Fanny's low social stratum is also reflected in her illiteracy; it is this handicap that allowed Mabel to take advantage of her. With her superior educational training, Mabel was able to convince Fanny that she had to take full blame for Pancho's death. Like Nélida's mother, Fanny also accepts her social position, although after Pancho became a policeman she hoped to marry him and better herself socially. At the spring dance where Fanny is treated like a lady, she reacts thus:

> [...] I dust the furniture with the feather duster, with a wet rag and soap I wash the floors, the soap and the scrubbing board are kept in the kitchen sink, he bought a gentleman's ticket for one peso, the orangeade was so refreshing, and I came as a lady and paid only twenty cents, the girls who go to the dance buy ladies tickets even though they are only maids, the same as the store clerks, dressmakers' assistants, or young ladies who are teachers... (pp. 86-87)

She experiences an exhilarating sense of psychological satisfaction since this is the only time when she can equate her social status to that of other ladies of higher social category. Fanny is the only female in the novel who does not do anything dishonest to elevate her social position. This is not to say that she did not want to better herself socially; on the contrary, she believed that a marriage to Pancho would genuinely enhance her situation. However, unlike Mabel, she really fell in love with Pancho and was completely honest and faithful to him. When Fanny discovers that Pancho is having an affair with her mistress, she stalks him as he leaves Mabel's bedroom and murders him. She then lies to the courts to save Mabel, and, by doing this, allows her to emerge totally unscathed from this incident. To the end we perceive Fanny as self-sacrificing and sincerely altruistic in her behavior.

Clearly Puig's presentation of Fanny constitutes his most serious criticism of the social milieu in Vallejos. Although she occupied the lowest rung in the social ladder, she is the most honest female in the novel. Even her assassination of Pancho was carried out because of her sincere love for him. This love, however, does not justify the crime, but the author succeeds in gaining the reader's sympathy for

Fanny by portraying Pancho as an irresponsible and uncaring man who took advantage of her solely to satisfy his sexual needs.

There is some poetic justice in the fact that Fanny emerges as the only happy female in the novel. Mabel, after an unhappy marriage, is retired but she has to work as a private tutor to help defray the medical expenses for her grandson who has been afflicted with infantile paralysis. Nélida has died, still loving Juan Carlos. Doña Leonor is sick and lives with her daughter, Celina. She lacks any visible or dependable means of financial support and is urging Celina to marry some wealthy person; her greatest fear is that Celina may die leaving her with absolutely no means of support. Celina is still single but has the reputation of sleeping with any available male. Fanny however has achieved some kind of economic status. She had married and is now a widow. The author presents a last glimpse of her when he says:

> The aformentioned Thursday, September 15, 1968, at 5:OO P.M., Antonia Josefa Ramírez was traveling by chaise from her farm to the business center of Vallejos, nine miles away. Her twenty-one-year daughter Ana María Lodiego was going with her. They would visit the stores to continue shopping for the girl's trousseau since she was soon to marry one of their neighbors, the owner of a milk farm [...] her greatest satisfaction lay in visiting her son Pancho, now settled in a newly built cottage. Fanny asked Ana María if it would be better to buy the sheets and towels at the Palomero House or at the Argentine Bargain Store. (pp. 221-222)

By presenting Fanny as the happiest and most prosperous of all the female protagonists, Puig underscores the hollowness and superficiality of the members of the bourgeois groups in Vallejos. Through Fanny and her subsequent elevated social status the novelist presents the reader with the most telling criticism of the hypocrisy and falseness of the artificially created social groups in Vallejos and of perhaps the whole of Argentina.

Besides stratifying and presenting a clear and critically panoramic view of the artificially created social divisions in Coronel Vallejos, Puig also provides descriptions and criticism of the social environment in the city of Buenos Aires. For example, both Mabel and Nélida move to the city with the hope of improving their social and economic status and both of them are unsuccessful. Mabel marries because she is getting older and fears being left out. She does not tell her fiancee about her previous sexual experiences with Juan Carlos. As she window shops in Nené's neighborhood she reflects that "perhaps any man who passed her on that street could give her more happiness than her dubious fiancee" (p.185). For Mabel Buenos Aires has not brought the happiness or economic stability she had expected. She hates life in the city and as she strolls in Nélida's neighborhood she mentally derides it. She thinks: In the mountains there (Córdoba) was the man who once had loved her, who had thrilled her as no one had. On that street in Buenos Aires the trees bowed low, both day and night. What useless humility, it was night, there was no sun, why bow? Had those trees forgotten all dignity and pride? (p. 185)

Mabel works in the Caballitos district as a teacher and in the evening has to take in private students to help pay the doctor for her grandson's illness. Life in the city has not fullfilled her social or financial expectations.

Nélida got married to Donato José Massa, an auctioneer and has also moved to Buenos Aires. Although she has two children, she is still in love with Juan Carlos. She lives in a cramped apartment with hardly any furniture; however, she lies about her economic state to her friends and relatives in Vallejos. She tells them that she lives in comfort and that she has acquired new furniture and electrical appliances and that she regularly visits the theatre. When Fanny visits Buenos Aires Nélida invents one excuse after another to prevent her from coming to her house and seeing the actual state in which she lives. Nélida is still keeping up false social appearances as she mistakenly believes that her self-appointed middle class status demands it.

Fanny, without Nélida's knowledge, decides to surprise her with a gift. She visits her and since Nélida is not at home, she is ushered into Nélida's apartment by the janitor. Later she calls her to ask her whether she liked the gift. Nélida makes her promise that she will not tell her mother about the condition of her apartment in Buenos Aires. Fanny agrees, not without first making her promise to give her some clothes for herself and for her baby, Panchito. After Nélida has finished talking to Fanny on the telephone, Puig takes us inside the apartment:

She again regrets having ordered a white telephone, always marked
by fingerprints. Besides she needs a chair in that room so she won't
have to sit on the bed each time she answers the phone [...] Going
toward the kitchen she crosses a room intended to be the dining
room where there's only a cardboard box containing a lamp with a
white tulle shade. In the small foyer, intended to be the living room,
there is also no furniture; she looks at the empty space wondering
if she will ever raise enough money to buy everything for cash,so that
she can avoid the extra charges for interest in installment plans. (pp.
139-14O)

By providing this clear description of the inside of Nélida's
apartment Puig forces us to discern the utter pretentiousness of her
life. Nélida is living a lie even here in the city. It is also not
unintentional that the author lets Fanny be the first one from
Vallejos to see the inside of Nélida's apartment. This is an ironic
twist as we know that Fanny has been relegated by the bourgeois in
Vallejos to the bottom rung of the social scale. It is then interesting
to note that it is she that Nélida has to bribe (with second hand
clothes) so that she may not describe Nélida's apartment to her
mother in Vallejos. This reversal of fortune allows the novelist to
make an important social commentary about the insincerity and
emptiness of the life of the members of the "wealthy" class in
Argentina. It is also to Fanny's credit that for her bribe she asks only
for used clothing for her son and then as an afterthought, for
herself.

It is again through Nélida that Puig comments on the society in
the city of Buenos Aires. In a letter to Juan Carlos's mother she
states:

How different it was in Vallejos! In the afternoon a girlfriend would
come, we would chat, listen to the serial, that is, before I worked at
the store, but here, what did I gain from coming to Buenos Aires?
I don't know anyone, the neighbors are a bunch of Italians just off
the boat, dead from the neck up, and a blonde who must be a kept
woman, my husband's positive. I don't know who I can talk to, to
nobody, and in the afternoons I try to sew a little and I watch over
these animals while they do their homework. Do you know what it's
like having two boys stuck in an apartment? They play with their toy
cars running races around the furniture. Just as well I don't have
good furniture yet, that's why I don't want to invite people from

> Vallejos to come visit, after they leave they criticize me for not having a fancy house, like it once happened already, I won't tell you who, where does it all get you? (p. 26).

Nélida's utter frustration with the city life is visible when she addresses her children as animals, locked up in an apartment. The smallness of the apartment serves as a suffocating prison which enhances her frustration with the coldness of the people of Buenos Aires. Puig again ridicules the hypocrisy of members of Nélida's social class when she criticizes her blonde neighbor, whom her husband Massa describes as a "kept woman." Nélida abhors living in close proximity to this woman and feels socially superior to her. To the reader this is a clear indication of Puig's sarcastic criticism since we know that Nélida herself was practically Nastini's "kept woman," a fact of which Massa her husband is apparently unaware. To assuage her frustration with the city Nélida asks Doña Leonor whether she should "find a young man who could give me a new life" (p.27). Like Mabel, Nélida is thinking about an extra-marital affair to compensate for her state of frustration at the people of the city.

Nélida decides to enroll her children in a club in Buenos Aires. Through her Puig again levels criticism on stratified Argentine society in Buenos Aires. She says:

> [...] The other day I saw such handsome boys, all at once, I hadn't seen a really handsome boy for such a long time and I went to sign the kids up at the club and there were boys there who looked like the ones at the Social Club. Of course they were under twenty five, and I am going to thirty. But what jerks they are at that club, you have to be presented by someone else they say, another member, but we hardly know anyone here in Buenos Aires. And I told my husband and he didn't even answer me, as if to say you are on your own. (p. 27)

The snobbishness of the members of this social club in Buenos Aires is the focus here of Nélida's frustation. Her children are refused membership as they had to be presented by another member. This evidently is the method the club adapts to segregate its membership and limit it to a certain restricted social group. Her search for social improvement in Buenos Aires is unsuccessful. It is clear that her life in the city is more frustrating and empty than it was in the provincial town of Vallejos.

Puig's motive for writing *Heartbreak Tango* was more than just for entertainment. A reading of the novel with Marx's concept of the rejection of the "art for art's sake" literary principle has demonstrated that one of the author's principal motives was to expose the hypocrisy, dishonesty and emptiness of a society which superficially and arbitrarily divides itself and which forces particular members of each social group to unscrupulously "claw" their way to the top. With the exception of Fanny, each individual's attempt to better himself socially is frustrated.

Fanny wants to ascend the social ladder by marrying Pancho the policeman, a man she genuinely loved. However, her love was not reciprocated and she suffered the humiliation of his disdain in the hope that a future legal liason with him was possible. When she kills him because of his infidelity, the reader finds himself hard-pressed to exhibit any kind of sympathy for him. At the end of the novel, Fanny is presented as the happiest female as she rides a chaise to buy her daughter's trousseau in one of Vallejo's most fashionable and expensive stores. Through her Puig says that economic prosperity is not a justifiable yardstick for division of social classes. He also destructively criticizes the emptiness and hypocrisy present in the life of the people who decide to segregate themselves from others whom they consider lower in economic position and education.

The Marxist literary concept which affirms that art does not exist solely for its own sake helps us better to understand the novel. Puig's criticism of the social divisions in Vallejos can be more clearly understood through an analysis of the narrative with this specific Marxist literary concept in mind. The social criticism that the novelist makes prompts the reader to perceive the artificiality and hollowness of the society in Vallejos and, to a lesser extent, of Buenos Aires. *Heartbreak Tango* is not "pure" art; it is instead a novel grounded on a Marxist social praxis which demands exposure and criticism of a society which adheres to rigid, artificial, social divisions.

A second characteristic of Marxist literary theory that will be employed to analyze and to better understand the text is Marx's concept of the function of reality in a work of art. From Chapter 1 we know that Marx believed that art reflects a social reality and demonstrates its salient features. Although political biases are part of the criteria for evaluating a work of art, neither Marx nor Engels believed that reality in a work of art encompasses a propagandistic perspective of the author's political beliefs. For them the novel is neither openly didactic nor does it offer solutions for the conflict it expreses. Reality for Marx and Engels dramatizes principal aspects of social life and since it does this, it can therefore portray man as polifaceted and contradictory: it can show a dichotomy between what the fictional character does and what he says; between what he is and what he appears to be and between what he does and what other characters force him to do.

About the portrayal of reality in *Heartbreak Tango* and in *La Traición de Rita Hayworth* (1968) Puig himself has stated:

> La primera novela era un intento de comprender por qué habían sucedido ciertas cosas; estaba todo centrado en mí como chico, después como adolescente. Los personajes de la novela son gente que había compartido algo conmigo en aquella época. Gente que había tenido muy cerca; familiares, vecinos [...] Gente que tenía tiempo para escucharme [...] La gente que tenía tiempo para escucharme estaba bastante desocupada. *La traición de Rita Hayworth* resulta una galería de desubicados, de gente que no encuentra su camino. De esa gente me animé a escribir porque losocía, habían estado más cerca mío, porque me habían dedicado tiempo. Pero quedaban en el tintero toda una cantidad de personajes de ese pueblo. Los que habían aceptado las reglas del juego, los que estaban en el "establishment" las "miss primavera," los profesionales [...] De ellos no me animé a escribir en *Rita Hayworth* porque consideraba que no tenía datos suficientes. No habían estado cerca mío. Pero me fascinaban como personajes. Terminada *Rita Hayworth* volví a la Argentina, en el año 67, y encontré después de muchos años a aquellos protagonistas, a esos integrados a la sociedad que me habían impresionado tanto. Estaban al témino de su trayectoria. Esa trayectoria me permitió reconstruir otros episodios, de finales del treinta y principios del cuarenta, la época en que había vivido con ellos en el pueblo. Al ver el punto de llegada de esa gente, toda muy frustrada, me animé a intentar escribir una novela, una interpretación de los hechos que me habían llenado de maravilla [....] De esa gente que había creído en los canones de una época, que habían aceptado las reglas del juego y les había ido, por lo general, muy mal. *Boquitas Pintadas* es un intento de comprender a esta gente en base a los datos que recogí al volver a mi país después de once años fuera [...] En la segunda novela intenté ya algún tramo en tercera persona, muy simple, aunque el

caracter omnisciente de esta técnica me seguía resultando sospechoso. En *Boquitas Pintadas* esa tercera persona es solo una especie de inventario de las acciones exteriores de los personajes.[2]

Both of Puig's novels [*Rita Hayworth* and *Boquitas Pintadas*] are grounded in a perceived and experienced reality and both novels reflect an empirical aspect of Puig's own reality. Clearly the novelist writes about typical people functioning under typical circumstances.

Puig, in *Heartbreak Tango*, writes about a reality which he lived through; that is, the reality of "Coronel Vallejos," which in actuality is a thinly disguised name for his own desolate home town of General Villegas. He further portrays reality in the novel when he states:

> Some of the characters in *Heartbreak Tango* have just one source of inspiration, one person who really existed; some are a combination, an alchemy of two or three people. All of the episodes really took place, maybe not in that order and not in the same household. But in that book, everything really happened at one time or another. The same is true about *Rita Hayworth*, where ninety-five per cent of the stuff is real and the other five per cent accounts for an added dash of pink I gave it to make all that blackness believable [...] If I had told things as they had happened, then no one would have accepted it as a reflection of reality. The reality of the pampas was much too dark to be believable.[3]

Puig believes that a linear historical narrative would have made the novel less readable and perhaps uninteresting. In *Heartbreak Tango* Puig combines a mythical character, Juan Carlos, with the stark reality of the life in the pampas to supply the readers with a credible and realistic account of the sordid realities of life in the provincial town of General Villegas. Puig accentuates this need for a combination of fiction (myth) with fact (reality) when he says that:

> People would say: oh, those books are just taped records of reality; you went out in the streets and recorded the voices of the people, that's all. That made me furious. Even if the characters' voices were the only material--and they were not--I was "editing" them just as other writers edit cultured, written language. This was a matter that I had made clear to myself from the first day that I started to write literature: the fact that I was dealing with reality wasn't enough;

reality had to be told in terms of beauty, otherwise there was no
satisfaction for me (Christ, pp. 55-56).

Puig believes that reality combines with beauty to make the work
of art credible. As he again asserts: "Los personajes [en *Boquitas
Pintadas*] existieron. Algunos de ellos no llegaron a conocerse, pero
pienso que si se hubiesen cruzado, podría haber sucedido lo que
sucede en la novela..."[4]

Reality is first expressed in the novel in the author's description
of life in Coronel Vallejos, the name he gives to his native General
Villegas. As Emir Rodríguez Monegal says:

> [...] Terminó (Puig) escribiendo uno en que los personajes de su vida
> real adquirirían proporciones de fábula y en que el desolado pueblo
> pampero que se llama General Villegas aparece metamorfoseado
> como "Coronel Vallejos" (Monegal, p. 26).

Puig takes an aspect of his past experiences and fictionalizes it
to make the story more credible. He describes the people of this
town both in *Rita Hayworth* and in *Heartbreak Tango*; in the
former he explains the life of the downtrodden while in the latter he
talks more about the life of the elite. In both cases he showcases life
in an actual provincial town, a life which forms part of his past and
therefore of an existing entity.

Another manner in which actual reality is depicted in the novel
is through Puig's description of a social phenomenon which exists in
many countries: that is, the belief that the cities offer more
economic and social opportunities than the smaller towns. This
belief causes the migration of many people from provincial towns
like Vallejos/Villegas to the metropolis. Since Latin-American
countries are generally poorer than North American countries, this
aspect of social reality is more pronounced in Latin America. Puig
clearly reflects this social predicament in *Heartbreak Tango*. He
depicts people functioning in the desolate environment of Vallejos
and reacting to it by migrating to Buenos Aires.

For example, both Mabel and Nélida travel to the capital to
better their lives and both are very unhappy in that environment.
Nélida longs for the life in Vallejos and criticizes the stagnant life in
Buenos Aires. By contrast Fanny has to stay in Vallejos as she has

no economic means that allow her to go to the city; ironically, she is the only woman who achieved happiness and some measure of economic prosperity, and she did not have to migrate to the city to accomplish them. Puig portrays this aspect of a Latin-American environment in the novel and clearly wants to convey the idea that economic prosperity and happiness are not always to be had in the city.

Yet another example of the reflection of reality in the novel is Puig's description of another aspect of a cultural trait that exists in Latin America. This cultural element is perhaps best articulated if we look at one example from Argentine history. It is a fact that Eva Duarte left the small provincial town of Junín to seek fame and fortune as an actress in the city. As we now know, she achieved fame and economic prosperity not as an actress but as the wife of Juan Perón (1895-1974). This Latin-American cultural practice through which the female believes that she can achieve some measure of ecomomic well-being and societal status only by depending on the man is amplified by Puig in the novel.

Women in this text are presented as weak, dependent and devoid of any significant measure of free will. They all aspire to a higher place in the social hierarchy and they all believe that this can be accomplished only if they marry someone in a higher social bracket. Mabel, for example, thinks of the economic and social advantages of marrying Borough-Croydon. The editor of *Feminine World* (incidentally also a woman) echoes her thoughts. Mabel schemes to marry Croydon and enjoy the wealth and status which this liason will bestow upon her; at the same time she decides to have Juan Carlos as a lover. Juan Carlos agrees with this plot as he will be appointed manager of one of Croydon's ranches and have easy access both to Mabel and to the boss's wealth, all at the same time.

A second example of this sociocultural behavioral pattern is refected in Nélida's personality. She wants to marry Juan Carlos and in this manner elevate her social status. She thinks that his death shatters this plan; in truth the reader is aware that Juan Carlos never planned to marry her. He regarded her as a sexual object to be discarded as soon as his lecherous intentions were satisfied. It is ironic that Nélida resisted having sex with him because she feared he would discover that she was not a virgin and, like a typical Latin macho, discard her.

Celina, Juan Carlos's sister, is a third example of this Latin-American cultural tradition. She attempts to better her socioeconomic status by marrying anyone (and she does not discriminate) who is above her economic niche. At the end of the novel we see her mother encouraging her to marry a doctor (she had been seen in his car) so that the daughter can better take care of her in her old age. Celina never marries but not for lack of trying; in truth nobody wants to marry her as she is visualized as the town prostitute since she has been seen in a number of men's vehicles.

Even Fanny does not escape this aspect of Latin-American culture. Like the other females in Vallejos, she believed that her economic and social level would be enhanced if she married Pancho, the father of her bastard child. She murders him because of his infidelity and ends up marrying a widower. In the final episodes of the novel Fanny is presented as economically prosperous and relatively happy. It is again deliberate that the author describes the woman who did not go to the city for fame and fortune as the wealthiest and happiest character in the novel.

Puig shows the women as typical provincial Latin-American females reacting in their typical and real environment. Like Evita they go (with the exception of Fanny) to the city to better themselves. They are however victims of their environmental reality. Unlike Eva, the females in the novel were not able to marry powerful and wealthy males. Their dreams are shattered and they end up as bitter and frustrated matrons thinking of having extra-marital affairs in the mistaken belief that this will spark their dreary existence in the city. Eva Duarte is therefore the exception and not the rule.

Puig further explores this cultural phenomenon in Latin America as he delineates the economic and social dependency of the females on the males. The women in the novel could not "pull themselves by their own bootstraps." They abandon the town to escape the social and environmental trap which it offers, without realizing that their dependency on their male couterparts is their trap and that a process of cultural re-education might be the only escape from their economic and social dependency. The novelist clearly adheres to the Marxist concept that society is reflected in a work of art as he distinctly portrays this cultural practice that still dominates a great part of the environment in contemporary Latin America.

A fourth manner through which empirical reality is shown in the novel is through the author's choice of an actual line from an existing popular Argentine song as the title of the novel. Here Puig enhances the proportional relationship between myth and reality and adds to the narrative's popularity and mass appeal. The book's title is derived from a popular foxtrot sung by a well-known Argentine singer named Carlos Gardel. This song was the title song of the movie called *El tango en Broadway,* and lines from it are repeated throughout the text. For example, the novel itself is divided into two parts, with the first section titled "A tango lingers on true red lips" and the second "a tango lingers on blue, violet, black lips." Both titles are lines from the Gardel song and are therefore reflections of a verifiable aspect of a popular Argentine culture.

Marxist criticism which seeks the reflection of realistic aspects of society in a work of art is also epitomized in Puig's *Heartbreak Tango* when the novelist, through introductions of lines and titles of foreign films and songs, criticizes contemporary Argentine and perhaps Latin-American society that emphasizes dependency on foreign consumer goods. To understand this specific portrayal of Marxist reality in this narrative, the reader must realize that Puig himself worked closely with the English translator of the novel.

In the original Spanish version, the author utilized popular lines from the tangos of Alfredo Le Pera. In the translation, however, Le Pera's lines were replaced with those of Homero Manzi. About this change the author says:

> Los tangos de Le Pera, descubrimos, son intraducibles. Su encanto está en las palabras, en el sonido de esas palabras muy musicales, mientras que las imágenes son muy flojas. Toda, toda la magia de Le Pera está en la elección de las palabras, que no se puede repetir en otro idioma. Pero Manzi, en cambio, tiene imágenes más fuertes que pasan mucho mejor en la traducción [...] Como he trabajado mucho con el lenguaje de mis personajes, he tenido, forzosamente, que trabajar con el cancionero de la época, con la radio de la época, grandes influencias en el lenguaje de esos personajes [...] Mis personajes son, por lo general, primera generación de argentinos que no hereda de sus padres un gran bagaje cultural. Esa primera generación tuvo que un poco inventarse el lenguaje; hubo que echar mano a modelos que estaban a mano. Los modelos más próximos eran la radio, las canciones, el tango; en los años cuarenta los boleros de México y Cuba; los subtitulos de las películas americanas

y mucho las revistas femeninas, las revistas de modas. (Sosnowski, pp. 79-80)

To portray a social reality, the author duplicated verifiable aspects of the surrounding environment as they were reflected in the popular songs, movies and magazines. It is evident that popular language was a tangible aspect of this ambience and through its utilization, the author anchors the novel in an existing social reality.

As he reflects this linguistic aspect of the culture in the text, the novelist also makes a critical Marxist comment about the Latin-American mentality which stresses that the utilization of foreign manufactured products (particularly North American) is the hallmark of high social status. The text contains numerous comments that show the high value that the Argentine bourgeoisie places on foreign manufactured products.

A few examples of these are: "As long as you can smile, success can be yours." (Radio commercial for toothpaste, Buenos Aires, 1947), (p. 21). "She fought with the fury of a tigress for her man! He treated her rough-and she loved it!" (ad for *Red Dust*, starring Jean Harlow and Clark Gable), (p. 32). "A woman's lips set the frozen north aflame." (tag line for *Northern Pursuit*, starring Errol Flynn and Julie Bishop), (p. 131). "I wish I could say I was sorry." (tag line for *The Letter*, starring Bette Davis), (p. 157). "It was the look in her eyes that made him think of murder." (tag line for *Woman in the Window*, starring Edward G. Robinson and Joan Bennett), (p. 187), and "She was one of the dreaded Cat People--doomed to slink and prowl by night...Fearing always that a lover's kiss might change her into a snarling, clawing killer!" (ad for *Cat People*, starring Simone Simon and Kent Smith), (p. 201).

By emphasizing the popularity of foreign-made films and consumer products, the novelist criticizes the Latin-American belief that locally produced consumer goods are inferior to the foreign ones, suggesting an imperialism of the mind perpetrated by the rich foreign countries to keep the Latin-American nations dependent on them.

A final example of the employment of the Marxist concept of reality in the novel is Puig's portrayal of "typical people under typical circumstances" in a work of art. In the novel, the author explains how people live their lives through the medium of the radio and the soap opera. The "radioteatro" is the cheapest and most common form of entertainment. The plot is very melodramatic and is hardly intellectually challenging. Soap operas are epitomes of fantasy and are removed from reality and from the occurrences of daily life. Yet the women from Vallejos live their lives according to the soap operas transmitted daily on the radio.

As an example, when Mabel visits Nélida in Buenos Aires she tells her about the new "radionovela" that details the emotional life of a wounded soldier and a young unhappily married lady who secretely cures him in her barn. Of course they fall in love and he has to leave. As Mabel and Nélida talk, the latter turns the radio on and in the background the reader hears that day's installment of the soap. The images portrayed in that day's episode   parallel Nélida's past life so closely that the reader, to avoid being confused, has consciously to separate fantasy from reality. Through this means Puig shows an anti-reality since he demonstrates how these people lived their real lives through an unreal and   fantasy-filled soap opera.

This "unreal reality" is distanced from the reader and appears incredible even though Puig himself admits that going to the cinema was one of his favorite activities in General Villegas and that it had a profound influence in his life and therefore was part of his own reality.   In a town where the avenues for cultural entertainment were limited, people were coerced to listen to soap operas and go to the movies. Hence in real life it was difficult to separate reality from the fantasy spewed out in the movies. In the novel the women fantasized about their men and compared them to the plastic heroes of the radio.

As an example, Juan Carlos was idealized by the women of Vallejos and his unnatural beauty was one of the major qualities that made him attractive to women. However, Juan Carlos was a thief, a gambler, and an irresponsible emotional cripple, yet all the women in the town loved him. They were mercilessly cruel to each other and blamed Juan Carlos's flaws on each other rather than on him. To them he was the celluloid hero from the "radionovelas" who could do no wrong. This "false reality" combines myth (fiction) with fact since it shows that the people in Vallejos (particularly the women) lived their real lives through the myth disseminated by the soap operas. As Alfred J. MacAdam says:

> *Boquitas Pintadas*, like *La traición*, represents a real world, a world
> devoid of history a world where time does not contain dialectical
> elements. This is the same as saying that in the rural Argentine world
> history does not exist, that the beings who live there live in a flux of
> time but that they never reach that level which separates a prehistoric
> state from an historical state. This does not mean that there is no rural
> Argentine history, but it does indeed imply that what has been called
> history is not real but a fiction. Manuel Puig has represented this false
> history.[5]

In the novel, the non-representation of history is realistic since
there was no history to represent. MacAdam calls this non-
representation of history a "false history" and states that Puig
presents this "false history" clearly in *Boquitas*.

Both Puig and Fuentes capture in their respective novels the
Marxist aspect of the presentation of reality in literature. The
description of "typical people under typical circumstances" facilitates
the comprehension of each of the novels since it makes the reader
more aware of the existence [in *Artemio*] or non-existence [in
Heartbreak Tango] of a historical reality which has a profound effect
on the lives of the protagonists.

Another characteristic of Marxist literary theory that will be
utilized in analyzing *Heartbreak Tango* is the concept of the
relationship of form and content in a work of art. To understand
this symbiotic reationship in the novel it is necessary to analyze
Puig's concepts on this theme. It is essential at this time to reiterate
the well-known fact that the problem of form and content in
literature has been one that has been studied and analyzed by many
literary critics. It is worth emphasizing here that a work of art can
not be considered Marxist simply because the author promulgates
some kind of proportional relationship between form and content.
It would therefore be a mistake to label *Heartbreak Tango* Marxist
simply because it may do this. Instead it will be shown that a reading
of the text with Marx's concept of the function of form and content
in mind will facilitate its understanding.

Puig himself addresses the issue of form/content in literature in
an interview with Danubio Torres Fierro. He says:

> Ante todo creo que nunca debo proponerme ilustrar una teoría. Eso
> nunca me interesó. Es el inconsciente el que va escribiendo y dictando.
> Toda esta teoría tan precaria que estoy tratando de exponer es

deducción, es posterior a la obra. En todas mis novelas he partido de la necesidad de contarme algo a mí mismo. Una historia o un tema me empieza a obsesionar y, a partir de ahí, escribo. Ese impulso me lleva a buscar una forma.[6]

Puig states that a theme or an aspect of history obsesses him then prompts him to search for a form, a vessel to express this obsessive content. He reiterates his belief in the primacy of content over form in an interview with Saul Sosnowski. He says:

"[...] A partir de *Boquitas*, he tratado de relatar en los términos que mejor se avinieran al contenido. El contenido-creo-debe siempre preceder a la forma" (Sosnowski, p.79).

Puig thus supports Marx's theory that the content determines the form
and that the latter is simply a vehicle to transmit the former.
Puig further amplifies his philosophy on the literary relationship between form and content in general and in *Heartbreak Tango* in particular in an interview with Emir Rodríguez Monegal:

ERM: La primera pregunta que se me ocurre hacerte es, muy obviamente: ¿Por qué elegiste el género folletinesco para tu última novela?
MP: Elegí el folletín como género literario porque se adecuada a la historia que tenía para contar. Por supuesto que primero encontré el tema; en una segunda etapa elegí la forma de narrarlo. Tomé el folletín por su estructura, muy atenta al interés narrativo; además son propios del folletín los personajes esquemáticos y la emotividad, elementos con que me interesaba trabajar (Monegal, p. 28)

The novelist further justifies his use of the soap opera form of narration in this novel when he says:

The story [*Heartbreak Tango*] was all about failure: the failure of people who had believed in all the lies of authority. And in the rhetoric of passion too. They had believed the words of the songs: love was something that everything else had to be sacrificed to. But, these middle-class people had not really acted according to passion. Their real attitude was a scheming one, a calculating one--a Catholic, middle class, cold approach to things, always directed to climbing a little further up on the social scale. As a matter of fact, they had betrayed their belief in passion by their conduct. So I thought it would be interesting to find a form that would contain that contradiction, to repeat the characters' contradiction in the form of the book. I considered the idea of using the structure of the serials but at the same time of sustaining it with a lot of realistic detail. So suspense and romance had to be emphasized, each chapter had to end at a crucial moment. I narrated by escamoteando, by palming some of the incidents--the way a magician does--and not revealing them in their proper chronological order-the tricks of the folletín. At the same time I thought of a very distant narrator--if there was a narrator at all-giving a disinterested, neutral, dispassionate approach to all this (Christ, p. 54).

In the novel itself the first example of the Marxist form/content theory of literature can be perceived in the narrative technique employed by the author. Let us examine this further. The novel is divided into two separate parts, with each section containing eight installments or "entregas." As in conventional soap operas, each installment is titled as an episode and not as a chapter. All the events related have occurred already and as in typical soap operas, the novel begins by reporting one of the principal elements of the plot: namely, the death of Juan Carlos. Although the reader is aware of his death, he is nevertheless intrigued by the effects that it had on other personalities in the novel. The reader is also responsible for piecing together a non-linear and non-chronologically related series of events. This non-traditional narrative structure epitomizes a significant aspect of the form and, as we will see, is intentionally crafted to embody a particular content.

Unlike Fuentes's *The Death of Artemio Cruz*, the content of *Heartbreak Tango* is not an empirically historical one. Indeed, Puig's novel has all the conventional elements of a trashy soap opera: there is intrigue, romantic love, jealousy and murder. The content is not difficult to grasp but the reader has to remain alert because of the narrative form utilized to articulate this soap-opera content. The episodic form adds to the "radioteatro" characteristic of the content; by dividing the novel into sixteen episodes the author makes it seem to have been mass produced for a consumer-oriented society. This episodic form denotes the author's technique of using the form to express the all-important content. He wants to expose the protagonists as vulgar, common and as "mass produced" in Argentine society. On the other hand, the imposition of this strict sixteen episode pattern of narrative structure superimposes some kind of order on the normally chaotic and seemingly disorganized narrative technique of the popular soap opera. This rigid (sixteen episodes) and organized form seems to be in contradiction to the chaotic and non-chronological "order" of the content. However a closer glance at the carefully regimented form reveals that it is the author's way of ridiculing the content. As we know, the novel describes the malicious manner in which people from a higher social hierearchy look down on those who are lower in the economic and social scale. Puig clearly states that this emphasis on "verticality" in society occurs both in the provincial towns and in the capital. The people are presented as disoriented, self-centered and confused as they "claw" their way from one social position to another. By articulating this content in a rigid sixteen-episode form Puig makes fun of the chaotic and goal-less life of the protagonists. The organized sixteen-episode form represents life as it should be rather than as it is chaotically presented in the novel. As Jonathan Tittler says: "[...] The form symbolizes the clearly defined perspective from which the shallow contents are exhibited; it is emblematic of the parody at work in these novels."[7]

Another aspect of the narrative structure that demonstrates that the content determines the form is through the "anchoring devices" which the author uses to provide the reader with information essential for an understanding of the plot. These devices are important if one considers the non-chronological description of the events. These anchoring devices permit the reader to be part of the content since they provide "windows" of information which are similar to the descriptions given by an omniscient narrator. Tittler calls these devices "verbal snapshots" and suggests that they place emphasis on static rather than on dynamic order. He (Tittler) provides an example from episode three of the novel (titled Picture Album) to illustrate this literary device:

The covers are in black and white cowhide, the pages of parchment paper. The first page is inscribed in ink: Juan Carlos Etchepare 1934, the second page is blank, and the third is covered with printed old-fashioned lettering interlaced with lances, lariats, spurs, and gaucho belts, forming the words ME AND MY PAMPAS. Next...(p.32)

The rest of the quotation (not quoted by Tittler) needs to be cited here since it serves, in this author's opinion, to further illustrate this literary device:

[...] the pages on the right are headed by a printed inscription, the ones on the left are not. Inscriptions: "Here I was born, wild pampas," "Dear old ma and pa," "The bad seed grows," "To school, rain or shine," "First communion: Christians yes! barbarians no!"... (p.32)

This static description of this photo album provides useful information about Juan Carlos's life. At first glance this description seems to serve no purpose but later on in the novel we realize its importance since it describes the intimate relationship between Juan Carlos and Mabel. It is indispensable for the reader to remember this "verbal snapshot" since it later proves essential in understanding the actions of Mabel. This aspect of the content (the reader's grasp of Mabel's emotional character) is later made more comprehensible by this apparently chronologically useless piece of information.

Tittler suggests that another anchoring or ordering device utilized by the novelist is the regular inclusion of certain key phrases or clauses. He suggests that an example of this occurs in the ninth episode which begins with the label "Recapitulation." After a brief plot summary, Tittler says that the heading January 27, 1938, appears followed by: "Taking a break in her day's activity, at 12:48 Nélida Enriqueta Fernández wiped her mouth with her napkin, folded it, and left the table with the purpose of taking an hour's siesta" (p.116). This section ends with two questions: "What in that moment was her greatest desire?" (p. 117) and "What in that moment was her greatest fear?" (p. 117). Tittler says that the subsequent part of the novel also begins with "On the aforementioned January 27, 1938, taking a break in the day's activity" (p.117). This section also ends with similar questions on Juan Carlos's desires and fears. As Tittler states, the third narrative sequence, which deals with Mabel, also begins with "On the aforementioned January 27, 1938, taking a break in the day's activity at 5:30 P.M..." (p.118). The fourth section on Pancho (p. 120) and the fifth dealing with Fanny (p. 121) all begin in the same manner and pose the same questions at the end.

Puig chooses this repetitious narrative form to express a linear and stable content and to represent the cyclical and boring activities in the provincial town of Vallejos. This repetitive form also successfully synchronizes the activities of these different protagonists and as Tittler says: "...lends a geometric, architectural quality to the text, which provides an almost tangible stability" (Tittler, p. 191). We can see in these examples from the narrative that the form reflects the preconceived content and that the consistently repetitive phrases are a formal tool to embody a stable and almost "tangible" content. As Lydia D. Hazera says:

> Puig's diverse narrative techniques combine to produce a forceful impact through parody, re-creation of social milieu, and psychological development. By harmoniously relating form, language and theme, Puig vividly portrays the drabness, pathos and conflicts of the young people. The impression is enhanced by his strong parody of language, close-up narrative frames, streams of sensory images and thoughts and shifting points of view, all contributing to a provocative collage of the social milieu and times in which the characters lived.[8]

Hazera asserts that the novelist combines a gamut of narrative forms to mirror the content that he portrays in the novel. By harmoniously relating form and theme (content), the writer provides a realistic picture of the environment and society in which the characters in the novel functioned.

A third literary device which the author uses in the narrative structure to show that the content determines the form is his use of the language. Talking to Ronald Christ about his utilization of the language in his novels Puig has said:

> PUIG: Well, let's say that in many cases I work with alienated languages. But then, what language is not alienated? I work with that stuff; it's my material. I agree with what Donoso says but one shouldn't forget that quite often, at a second stage, I cut that stuff to measure, which implies a transformation. Anyhow, I believe I've always used those degraded languages in order to make them significant, to turn them into signs, if I may use an impressive word. It may be a way of

putting them at the service of literature or vice versa. Both literature and those languages should gain by the operation (Christ, p. 58).

Puig affirms that he uses degraded language as "signs" to serve literature. In the following paragraphs we will see how he manipulates the language as a literary means to establish a Marxist relationship between form and content.

In the novel Puig utilizes the language at various levels: he employs the artificial and expressive language of the "radioteatro;" he also uses the popular and emotionally-charged dialect of the tango and the practical and dispassionate discourse of the newspapers and of the police reports. Puig also uses the language as signifiers or "signs" that represent a deeper mental process of the protagonist or that symbolize a more iconic aspect of the environment being described. A few textual examples will illustrate his use of this literary device.

The first example occurs with his description of Juan Carlos, the main character in the narrative. Juan Carlos is a physically beautiful being who possesses all the classical attributes of any number of nineteenth century Romantic heroines: he is very handsome, pampered by his mother and sister and belongs (at least in Vallejos) to the middle class. Although Juan Carlos suffers from tuberculosis, his arrogant, dishonest and "machista" personality prevents the readers from feeling any sympathy for him, as they normally would for any one who is terminally ill.

It is deliberate that Puig presents Juan Carlos as the stereotypical Latin *male*, yet he has the physical attributes of a *female* protagonist of the nineteenth century novel. Like Benito Pérez Galdós's (1843-1920) *Doña Perfecta* (1876), Juan Carlos possesses a certain physical beauty, and like her he is sneaky, conniving, treacherous and manipulative. Unlike Doña Perfecta he is a man, and in this fashion the author parodies and ridicules the traditional perception of the typical Latin-American male.

Juan Carlos's sickness and his deprecatory attitude towards women also mock the conventional perception we have of the historical Don Juan. Whatever he was, the classical Don Juan was not a thief or a gambler or a man who schemed to get into bed with women just for the sake of their wealth or for a chance to improve his social status. As we can clearly see, in Juan Carlos Puig parodies the traditional Latin "macho" and criticizes the females who would fall for a pseudo Don Juan embodied in the person of Juan Carlos.

Juan Carlos's name obviously pokes fun at the name (Don Juan) of the mythical Spanish hero. Again, Puig uses the language ironically to ridicule the donjuanesque perception that Latin-American women have of typically handsome men like Juan Carlos. The classical Don Juan is always consistently presented as well groomed, mannerly, well educated and quite articulate. The paradoxical Don Juan (Carlos) that Puig presents has poor manners, associates with gamblers, is a thief and is semi-illiterate.

Examples of his poor education are shown through the abundance of orthographic errors he commits in his letters to his various lovers. Excerpts from a couple of these will suffice to illustrate his lack of formal education.

In one letter dated August 31, 1937 Juan Carlos says: "...The old lady wants me personally to take charge of dealing with the *tenents* in the two houses to try to *raize* the rent..." (p. 1O6) and "...The people at my *ofice* don't want to extend my *leeve*, what's it to them, it's without salary anyway..."(p. 1O7)

In these two portions of Juan Carlos's letters (italicized words are mine) we perceive the novelist's deliberate use or misuse of the language to denote a serious lack of academic training in Juan Carlos's upbringing. Lack of education infringes on his ability to correctly articulate his thoughts and results in a stilted and disconnected prose. The author wants the reader to imagine this character as semi-literate and as deprived of the aesthetic veneer that a sound education provides. As we realize, he does this through Juan Carlos's stunted prose which is a result of his lack of knowledge of correct rules of orthography. The content (Juan Carlos's poor academic background) is therefore clearly expressed in the form (his misuse of the language).

Another example of Puig's use of the language to demonstrate the Marxist literary concept of the relationship between form and content can be observed when he employs words as signifiers or signs for a psychological process or as symbols of a deeper undercurrent of action in an environment. The utilization of the language in this particular manner has been done by diverse writers (example García Lorca (1899-1936)) and is not by itself a characteristic of Marxist literary theory; rather it is one of the diverse literary recourses employed by the narrator as he adapts the Marxist concept of the predominance of content over form in *Heartbreak Tango*. Illustrations from the text will make this clear.

The first example centers around the description of Juan Carlos's disease. Throughout the novel the reader is made aware that Juan Carlos suffers from tuberculosis; however, the disease itself is never mentioned by name. It is insinuated and hinted at (Mabel perhaps comes the closest when she says that Juan Carlos suffers from "continual colds and often feels tired," (p. 37) and "from the beginnings of a certain highly contagious illness." (p. 4O)). Puig uses this refusal to call the disease by name to expose the Latin American's inbuilt penchant to hedge away from reality. By refusing to mention the name of the sickness, the person hopes that it will dissipate of its own volition. In Latin America, similar mental attitudes are exhibited towards political problems and towards social "problems" like homosexuality. To the typical Latin American, acceptance of any "abnormal" phenomena is symptomatic of weakness and any sign of weakness is not socially accepted in a society dominated by the "macho" mentality. Juan Carlos is presented as the archetype of this "macho" syndrome and as such can not accept the existence of his sickness even when he starts spitting blood into his handkerchief. One can speculate that if Juan Carlos had managed to overcome this inborn resistance towards the acceptance of any kind of debility, then in all probability he might have sought help in the initial stages of the disease and perhaps have been cured.

In this fashion Puig uses the protagonists' refusal to mention Juan Carlos's sickness by name as a symbol of a far deeper Latin-American character flaw, a flaw that he speculates is embedded in Latino cultural heritage and that has to be overcome if a search for identity is to achieve some measure of success.

Yet another example of the use of the language as a symptom of a deeper psychological undercurrent in the text occurs when Puig employs the physically unhealthy state of Juan Carlos as a visible sign of the unhealthy status of Vallejos. The progressively rotting stages of Juan Carlos's tubercular lungs are emblematic of the putrification of the society in this provincial town. We perceive herein another use of the language as a sign of a more penetrating social malaise. An example of this particular usage of the language is evident in the description of the fig trees in the courtyard of Mabel's house. The author uses the fig trees as an example of pathetic fallacy to represent Pancho's lust for Mabel.

On page 140 Mabel invites Pancho to pick some ripe figs from the tree in her yard (it is to be remembered that her house is adjacent to the police station). Pancho agrees and it is during their conversation, which is heavily laced with sexual innuendos, that they decide that he will visit her at night after her mother is asleep. Ostensibly Pancho is supposed to jump into Mabel's yard and pull the ripe figs for her; however we know that the use of the double entendre is a superficial cover for the beginning of Pancho's and Mabel's illicit affair. Later on as Pancho consummates his relationship with Mabel, he uses the symbol of the fig as representative of his sexual mastery of her when he says "...the ripe fig, its green skin has no taste, inside the red pulp with its drops of honey, I ate all I wanted, down the hatch, the dolls on the shelf, natural hair and eyes that move..." (p. 153). From this quotation we see Puig's employment of the language as a signifier of Pancho's self-conceived notion of sexual and social superiority as he illicitly copulates with Mabel.

The author continues the symbolic uses of the fig tree as an iconic representation of a more penetrating sickness when he makes it representative of the death and life of nature. Towards the end of the novel there is a static description of Pancho's tomb. After detailing such descriptive characteristics as the open common grave, the linen that covered the bodies and Pancho's skeleton, the novelist says:

> [...] The common grave was located at the back of the cemetery [...] different types of weeds grew around it [...] the cemetery, far from the rest of town, had the form of a rectangle [...] The nearest fig tree could be found on a farm situated a little less than a mile away, and given the time of the year, it was covered with light green buds. (p. 221)

Pancho's cadaver, in contrast to the budding fig tree, is symbolic of the cyclical characteristic of nature: as Pancho's body rots, life begins with the tiny green buds of the fig trees. Nature therefore renews itself as life in Vallejos (symbolized by Pancho's body) disintegrates into nothing.

A final utilization of the language as a sign of a deeper social undercurrent occurs when Fanny murders her ex-lover Pancho as he surreptitiously exits from Mabel's bedroom. Like a predator, Fanny stalks him and stabs him several times with a long-bladed kitchen knife. The fact that Puig chose a knife as the murder weapon is deliberate: it is symbolic of the penis, which demonstrates that Pancho died because he literally gave his penis to somebody else. It is ironic that he had just come from sexually penetrating Mabel only to be penetrated himself by a pseudo penis. His sexual penetration of Mabel had resulted in a pleasureable, vindictive and bitter-sweet sexual death; by contrast, his immediate penetration at the hands of Fanny resulted, literally, in his painful death. In asserting that Pancho died because of his penis, the writer again criticizes the Latin-American "macho" mentality which dictates that a tangible sign of manhood is to "penetrate" as many women as possible, be it in or out of wedlock. Puig tells us that this "manly" attitude towards sex and sexual roles is not valid and can lead to emotional and moral chaos and confusion and in Pancho's case, even death.

Puig uses the language as a vehicle to convey the content and to make critical statements on diverse Latin-American social practices. For example, the deaths of Pancho, Nélida and Juan Carlos do not evoke in the reader the slightest sympathy. The writer uses death to unify the content as he demonstrates that each death is deserved. Even death is therefore symbolic of a deeper moral undercurrent since the novel points out that death is a just punishment for the wrongdoers of this world as exemplified by the deserved deaths of Pancho and Juan Carlos. About the unifying role of the language Severo Sarduy says:

> [...] lo que en él [el lenguaje] se subraya es su carácter de vehículo, de medio de transmisión y soporte de ideas recibidas; el de la frase, el volumen que definen las artistas sintácticas es el del lugar común: núcleo mitológico, estampa elaborada, eidos popular, concreción de fantasmas colectivas, situación codificada: sitio de encuentro.[9]

For Sarduy the language in *Heartbreak*...plays a pivotal role in unifying all the narrative elements in the novel.

A final method used in the narrative technique to support the Marxist literary concept that affirms that the content comes before the form is evident in the cinematographic techniques that the novelist employs in the novel. Puig intercalates these techniques with narrative methods employed in the "radioteatro" and in the newspapers and pulpy magazines. In this text two of the salient techniques of the movie camera that he employs to relate the novel and to adapt the form to the previously conceived content will be discussed.

Phyllis Mitchell suggests that the first cinematographic technique juxtaposes a mixture of interior monologues, flashbacks and seemingly disassociated thoughts to provide cinematic "closeups" ranging from short descriptive paragraphs to longer descriptions of a specific day in the life of a character. This technique is instrumental in showing the protagonists as patterning their lives on that of the celluloid heroes. The detailed cinematographic closeups present the characters in Vallejos as living their real life through the unreality presented in the cinema and in the "radioteatros." Mitchell calls this phenomenon "life by proxy" and suggests that the characters substitute themselves for stars in the film to achieve quick gratification. She says that the protagonists believe that their own lives should mirror the lives of the plastic heroes and if they do not then they think of themselves as failures.[10] An example of this technique will illustrate the use of this form to mirror the content.

The fourth episode (p.45) begins with: "Thursday, April 23, the sun rose at 5:50 A.M. Light winds blew from north to south, it was partly cloudy, with the temperature at 57 degrees Farenheit. Nélida Enriqueta Fernández slept till 7:45 A.M..."

The rest of the long descriptive paragraph provides a minute by minute account of Nélida's day. It details her aspirations as she dreams of marriage to Juan Carlos. The account of Nélida's day is closely followed by an equally long description of Juan Carlos's day and this is followed in the fifth episode (p.59) by long descriptive paragraphs which describe a day in the life of Mabel and then of Pancho and finally of Fanny.

These closeups which Judith A. Weiss describes as "blow by blow"[11] provide the reader with a compacted prose which closely imitates the panoramic closeups of the movie camera and gives a vivid, lucid and comprehensive overview of the content which in this case are the aspirations, ambitions and thoughts of the five major protagonists of the novel. This cinematographic technique is repeated throughout the novel and is an effective narrative form utilized by the novelist to portray the content.

A second narrative form that is taken from the cinema is reflected in the novelist's juxtaposition of phrases beside the actual words of the speaker to convey to the reader the person's thought as he speaks. Puig employs italics to show the person's thoughts and this allows the reader to understand the pattern of behavior exhibited by some of the characters. The most effective usage of this narrative technique occurs on page 143-144, during Mabel's and Pancho's "courtship." In the following excerpt I have put the italicized sections from the text in parentheses. Mabel starts the conversation.

-Yes, mama's always here, she almost never goes out.
-Then...when can I come down? [at night, at night...]
-[at night, at night...] I don't know, mama's in all the time...
-But at night she must sleep...[I don't make noise when I jump over the wall, the hens aren't going to wake up]
-Yes, but at night you can't see well enough to climb the tree. [a husky guy like him can climb a fig tree like nothing]
-I can see...
-But you can't see which fig is ripe, and which isn't. [come, come]
-By twelve for sure she's asleep...[I wonder if he raped Fanny, is he as strong as that? Fanny comes and finds me with a dark half-breed bum]
-Then I'm coming tonight at that time. [the runt's fianceé]

The use of this form of narration provides an insight into the thought process of both Pancho and Mabel. Although both parties do not engage in an open conversation about sex, the innuendos gleaned from their thought process (here shown in parentheses) as shown through this form of narration makes the dialogue so sexually charged that the reader is immediately cognizant of the fact that both Pancho and Mabel have tacitly agreed to engage in an illicit and underhanded sexual affair-she the delicate fig and he the husky guy who will metaphoriclly climb the fig tree. The fact that Mabel feels superior to Pancho is quickly substantiated when she conceives of him as "a half-breed bum." For Pancho the affair will establish his sexual superiority over her since he thinks of her fiancée as "a runt."

This form of narration, common to the cinema and to pulpy magazines, establishes the firm utilization of the Marxist concept of the primacy of the content to the form and is instrumental in helping the reader to better understand the psychological make-up of the protagonists of *Heartbreak Tango*. To conclude, it has to be emphasized that this Marxist analysis of this text does not suggest that the novel is a Marxist novel or that the author is Marxist. Rather, it demonstrates that a Marxist *reading* of the novel provides a better comprehension of the socioeconomic content of *Heartbreak*...since it allows the reader to utilize a different critical approach when he reads it. By utilizing the Marxist literary concepts of the negation of the principle of "art for art's sake," of the portrayal of reality in a work of art and of the superiority of content over form I hope to present the reader with a different and new method of perceiving this novel.

CONCLUSION

It is imperative at this stage to reiterate the purpose in writing this text. By no means was it meant to suggest or to imply that any of the three novels analyzed is Marxist or that any of the authors are Marxist. If one were to set out to write a novel with the explicit purpose of delineating the Marxist theory of literature as explained in Chapter 1 of this text, then the product itself would be propagandistic and anti-Marxist, for Marx himself did not consider literature which extolled a particular political concept or a specific literary theory as good literature.

The main purpose of this book is to demonstrate that one can gain heretofore unexplored insights into each of the respective author's purpose in writing their novels if one reads them with selected aspects of Marxist literary theory in mind. It is suggested that this will enable the reader to better understand the critical content of each of the narratives.

For example, in analyzing Vargas Llosa's *The Green House* the following principles of Marxist literary theory were utilized: (1) Marx's literary concept which affirms the portrayal of verifiable historical events in a work of art; (2) his description of the relationship between the economic base and the superstructure and (3) Marx's principle of literature which declares that in a work of art the content has primacy over the form. These three selected traits of Marxist literary theory do not make the novel Marxist; however they do help the reader to grasp the deeply socioeconomic content of the narrative since they facilitate comprehension of the historical reasons which explain the impoverished state of the great majority of the population in Iquitos and Piura.

Similarly, the selected characteristics of Marxist literary theory (for example the portrayal of a verifiable historical reality in literature and the negation of "art for art's sake") help illuminate both Fuentes's *The Death of Artemio Cruz* and Puig's *Heartbreak Tango*.

In Fuentes's novel the Marxist principles of literature that were chosen clearly illuminate the deeply historical content. By reading *The Death of Artemio Cruz* with Marx's form/content literary concept in mind, the reader can better understand the social and economic dislocation caused by the Mexican elite whom Fuentes depicts as traitors of the ideals of the 1910 Mexican Revolution.

In the same fashion, a reading of Puig's *Heartbreak Tango* with Marx's negation of the principle of "art for art's sake" in mind helps clarify the sociological criticism that he makes in the novel. This aspect of Marxist literary criticism illuminates the content of the novel as it permits the readers to grasp the devious machinations that people in Coronel Vallejos [alias General Villegas] practice in their selfish and frantic attempts to "claw" their way up the social ladder.

The three novels studied in this analysis describe specific Latin-American environments and detail the reactions of particular people living within these specific environments. It is therefore logical that an understanding of the novels presupposes some kind of understanding of the ambience in which they were written. A Marxist reading of these novels provides some knowledge and understanding of this environment since it supplies the critical literary tools that allow the reader to better analyze them.

Dr. Víctor Manuel Durán

Millikin University, June, 1993

NOTES

Introduction

1

Judy Kay Ferguson-Salinas, *Social reform in works of Carlos Fuentes*, Ph. D. dissertation, University of Oklahoma, 1970.

2

Luis Manuel Villar, *Carlos Fuentes: Literatura y Sociedad*, Ph.D. dissertation, University of Wisconsin, Madison, 1982.

3

Ileana Araujo, "Valores temáticos y estructurales en *La Muerte de Artemio Cruz*," *Caribe* 2 (1972): 85-95.

4

Linda S. Glaze, "La distorsión temporal y las técnicas cinematográficas en *La Muerte de Artemio Cruz*," *Hispamérica* 14, No. 40 (April, 1985): 115-120.

5

M.J. Fenwick, *Dependency Theory and Literary analysis: Reflections on Vargas Llosa's "The Green House"* (Minneapolis: Institute for the Study of Ideologies and Literature, 1981).

6

José Miguel Oviedo, *Mario Vargas Llosa: La invención de una realidad* (Barcelona: Barral Editors, 1977).

7

Michael Moody, "The web of defeat: A thematic view of characterization in Mario Vargas Llosa's *La Casa Verde*," *Hispania* 59: 11-23.

8

Marvin Lewis, *From Lima to Leticia: The Peruvian novels of Mario Vargas Llosa* (Lanham, Maryland: University Press of America, 1983).

9

Emir Rodríguez Monegal, "El folletín rescatado," *Revista de la Universidad de México* 27, No. 2 (1972).

1O

Phyllis Mitchele, "The Reel against the Real: Cinema in the novels of Guillermo Cabrera Infante and Manuel Puig," *Latin American Literary Review* 3, No. 5 (1974).

11

Jonathan Tittler, "Order, Chaos and Re-order: The novels of Manuel Puig," *Kentucky Romance Quarterly* 3O, No. 2 (1983).

12

Severo Sarduy, "Notas a las notas...A propósito de Manuel Puig," *Revista Iberoamericana* 37 (1971).

Chapter 1

1

Henri Arvon, *Marxist Esthetics*, trans. Helen Lane (London: Cornell University Press, 1973).

2

Quoted in Stanley Edgar Hyman, "The Marxist Criticism of Literature," *Antioch Review* 7 (1947): 545.

3

Quoted in Lee Baxandall and Stefan Morawski, ed., *Marx and Engels on Literature and Art: A selection of Writings* (St. Louis: Telos Press, 1973), pp. 115-116.

4

Quoted in Peter Demetz, *Marx, Engels and the Poets: Origins of Marxist Literary Criticism*, trans., Jeffrey L. Simmons (Chicago: The University of Chicago Press, 1967), p. 142.

5

Quoted in Terry Eagleton, *Marxism and Literary Criticism* (Los Angeles: University of California Press, 1976), p. 21.

6

Quoted from Mikhail Lifshitz, *The Philosophy of Art of Karl Marx*, trans., Ralph B. Winn (London: Pluto Press, 1973), p. 43.

Chapter 2

1

Mario Vargas Llosa, *La Casa Verde*, trans., Gregory Rabassa (New York: Harper and Row Publishers, 1968).

2

Mario Vargas Llosa, *Historia Secreta de una Novela* (Barcelona: Tusquets Editor, 1971), pp. 11-14.

3

M.J. Fenwick, *Dependency Theory and Literary Analysis: Reflections on Vargas Llosa's "The Green House"* (Minneapolis: Institute for the Study of Idelogies and Literature, 1981). All further references to this text will be from this edition and will be indicated by page numbers.

4

José Miguel Oviedo, *Mario Vargas Llosa: La invención de una realidad* (Barcelona: Barral Editors, 1977), p. 155.

5

Carlos Fuentes, *La Nueva Novela Hispanoamericana* (México: Editorial Joaquín Mortiz, S.A., 1969),p. 46

Chapter 3

1

Carlos Fuentes, *La Muerte de Artemio Cruz*, trans., Sam Hileman (New York: Farrar, Straus and Company, 1964). All further references to this text will be from this edition and will be indicated by page numbers.

2

Lee Baxandall, "An interview with Carlos Fuentes," *Studies on the Left* 3 (August 10, 1962): 49-50.

3

Luis Harss and Barbara Dohmann, "Carlos Fuentes, or the New Heresy," *Into the Mainstream: Conversations with Latin-American Writers* (New York: Harper and Row, 1967), p. 306.

4

From Claude Couffon, "Carlos Fuentes y la novela Mexicana," *Cuadernos congreso por la libertad de la cultura* (mayo-junio de 1960): 69.

5

Luis Manuel Villar, *Carlos Fuentes: Literatura y Sociedad* (P.hd. diss., University of Wisconsin-Madison, 1982), pp. 268-269.

6

Epifanio San Juan Jr., "Art against Imperialism," *Art in Society* 2: 222.

7

Carlos Fuentes, "Mexico: Children of the Revolution, the angry young men," *Look*, July 18, 1961, p. 34.

8

Klaus Meyer-Minnemann, "*La Muerte de Artemio Cruz*: Tiempo cíclico e historia del México Moderno," *Simposio Carlos Fuentes* 2: 89

9

Bienvenido de la Fuente, "*La muerte de Artemio Cruz*: Observaciones sobre la estructura y sentido de la narración en Primera Persona," *Explicación de textos literarios* 6 (1978):144-145.

10

Gerald W. Petersen, "Punto de vista y tiempo en *La muerte de Artemio Cruz de Carlos Fuentes*," *Revista de Estudios Hispanos* 7 (enero, 1972): 85-95.

11

Ileana Araujo, "Valores temáticos y estructurales en *La muerte de Artemio Cruz*," Caribe 2 (1977): 69-75.

12

Ethel Hammerly, "Estructura y sentido en *La muerte de Artemio Cruz de Carlos Fuentes*", *Explicación de textos literarios* 4: 207-212.

13

Hayden White, "The Fictions of Factual Representation," *The Literature of Fact*, ed., Angus Fletcher (New York: Columbia University Press, 1976), pp. 31-32.

14

Carlos Fuentes, *La nueva novela Hispanoamericana* (México: Joaquín Mortíz, 1969), pp.94-95. All other references to this text shall be shown by page numbers only.

15

Quoted in Araujo, p. 71.

16

Quoted in Hammerly, p. 2O9.

17

Carlos Fuentes, "A Life," The New York Review of Books (June 25, 1964) : 3.

Chapter 4

1

Manuel Puig, *Boquitas Pintadas*, trans., Suzanne Jill Levin (New York: Vintage Books, 1973). All further references to this text will be from this edition and will be indicated by page numbers.

2

Saul Sosnowski, "Entrevista con Manuel Puig," *Hispamérica* 3 (1973): 73-74.

3

Ronald Christ, "An interview with Manuel Puig," *Partisan Review* 44 (1977) : 54-55.

4

Emir Rodríguez Monegal, "El folletín rescatado," *Revista de la Universidad de México* 27, No. 2 (1972): 26.

5

Alfred J. MacAdam, "Manuel Puig's Chronicles of Provincial Life," *Revista Hispánica Moderna* 36 (197O) : 63.

6

Danubio Torres Fierro, "Conversación con Manuel Puig: La redención de la cursilería," *Eco* 28 (1975): 51O.

7

Jonathan Tittler, "Order, Chaos and Re-order: The novels of Manuel Puig," *Kentucky Romance Quarterly* 30, No. 2 (1983): 188.

8

Lydia D. Hazera, "Narrative Techniques in Manuel Puig's *Boquitas Pintadas* (Painted Little Mouths)," *Latin American Literary Review* 2, No. 3 (Fall/Winter, 1973) : 52-53.

9

Severo Sarduy, "Notas a las notas...A propósito de Manuel Puig," *Revista Iberoamericana* 37 (1971):562

10

See Phyllis Mitchelle, "The Reel against the Real: Cinema in the novels of Guillermo Cabrera Infante and Manuel Puig," *Latin American Literary Review* 11 (1977): 27.

11

Judith A. Weiss, "Dynamic correlations in Heartbreak Tango," *Latin American Literary Review* 3, No. 5 (1974) : 137-141.

BIBLIOGRAPHY

Araujo, Ileana. "Valores temáticos y estructurales en La Muerte de Artemio Cruz." Caribe 2 (1977): 69-75.

Arvon, Henri. Marxist esthetics. Translated by Helen Lane. London: Cornell University Press, 1973.

Baxandall, Lee. "An interview with Carlos Fuentes. "Studies on the Left 3 (August 1O, 1962): 48-56.

Baxandall, Lee and Morawski, Stefan, eds. Marx and Engels on Literature and Art: A selection of writings. St. Louis: Telos Press, 1973.

Boldori, Rosa. Mario Vargas Llosa y la literatura en el Perú de hoy Santa Fé, Artgentina: Colmenga, 1969.

Cano Gaviria, Ricardo. El buitre y el ave fénix: Conversaciones con Mario Vargas Llosa. Barcelona: Anagrama, 1972.

Carballo, Emmanuel. Diecinueve protagonistas de la literatura Mexicana del Siglo XX. México: Empresas Editoriales, 1965.

Christ, Ronald. "An interview with Manuel Puig." Partisan Review 44 (1977): 52-61.

Collier, Richard. The River that God Forgot. New York: E. P. Dutton and Co., Inc., 1968.

De la Fuente, Bienvenido. "La muerte de Artemio Cruz: Observaciones sobre la estructura de la narración en Primera Persona." Explicación de Textos Literarios 6 (1978): 143-151.

Demetz, Peter. Marx, Engels and the Poets: Origins of Marxist Literary Criticism. Translated by Jeffrey L. Sammons. Chicago: The University of Chicago Press, 1967.

Diez, Luis Alfonso. Mario Vargas Llosa's Pursuit of the Total Novel. Cuernavaca, México: CIDOC, 197O.

Eagleton, Terry. Marxism and Literary Criticism. Los Angeles: University of California Press, 1976.

Faris, Wendy B. "Desyoización: Joyce, Cixous/Fuentes and the
multivocal text." <u>Latin American Literary Review</u> 9-19
(Fall/Winter 1981): 31-39.

Fenwick, M. J. <u>Dependency Theory and Literary Analysis:
Reflections on Vargas Llosa's "The Green House."</u>
Minneapolis: Institute for the Study of Ideologies and Literature, 1981.

Ferguson-Salinas, Judy Kay. <u>Social Reform in selected works of
Carlos Fuentes</u>. Ph. D. dissertation, University of Oklahoma, 1970.

Franco, Jean. "Dependency Theory and Literary History: The case of Latin
America." <u>The Minnesota Review</u> 5 (Fall 1975, Special Supplement) :
1973-1975.

Fuentes, Carlos. <u>La nueva novela Hispanoamericana</u>. México:
Editorial Joaquín Mortíz, S.A., 1969.

----------. <u>La muerte de Artemio Cruz</u>. Translated by Sam Hileman. New
York: Farrar, Straus and Company, 1964.

Giacoman, Helmy F. <u>Homenaje a Vargas Llosa</u>. Long Island City:
Las Américas, 1972.

Hammerly, Ethel. "Estructura y sentido en <u>La Muerte de Artemio
Cruz</u> de Carlos Fuentes." Explicación de Textos Literarios 4: 207-212.

Hamilton, Carlos D. "La novela actual de Hispanoamérica." <u>Cuadernos
Americanos</u> 2 (marzo-abril 1973): 223-251.

Harss, Luis and Dohmann, Barbara.   <u>Into the Mainstream:
Conversations with Latin-American Writers</u>. New York: Harper and Row,
1967.

Hazera, Lydia D. "Narrative Techniques in Manuel Puig's <u>Boquitas
Pintadas</u>." <u>Latin American Literary Review</u> 2, No. 3 (Fall/Winter, 1973):
45-53.

Hyman, Stanley Edgar. "The Marxist Criticism of Literature."
<u>Antioch Review</u> 7 (1947): 545-568.

Jameson, Fredric. <u>Marxism and Form</u>. Princeton: Princeton
University Press, 1971.

Lifshitz, Mikhail. The Philosophy of Art of Karl Marx.
Translated by Ralph B. Winn. London: Pluto Press, 1973.

MacAdam, Alfred J. "Manuel Puig's Chronicles of Provincial Life."
Revista Hispánica Moderna 36 (1970-1971): 61-66.

Martín, José Luis. La narración de Vargas Llosa: Acercamiento
estilístico. Madrid: Gredos, 1974.

Marx, Karl and Engels, Friedrich. The German Ideology, Parts 1 & 111.
Edited by R. Pascal. New York: International Publishers, 1974.

----------. On Art and Literature. Moscow: Progress Publishers, 1976.

Marx, Karl. Capital. Vol. 1: The Process of Capitalist
Production. New York: International Publishers, 1967.

----------. Economic and Philosophic Manuscripts of 1844. Moscow:
Foreign Language Publishing House, 1959.

Meyer-Minnemann, Klaus. "La Muerte de Artemio Cruz: Tiempo
cíclico e historia del México Moderno." Simposio Carlos Fuentes 2: 87-98.

Mitchele, Phyllis. "The Reel against the Real: Cinema in the novels of
Guillermo Cabrera Infante and Manuel Puig." Latin American Literary
Review 11 (1977): 22-29.

Monegal, Emir Rodríguez. "El folletín rescatado." Revista de la
Universidad de México 27, No.2 (1972): 26-30.

Oviedo, José Miguel. Mario Vargas Llosa: La Invención de una
Realidad. Barcelona: Barral Editors, 1977.

Peck, David. "The New Marxist Criticism." Massachussetts Review 14:
639-647.

Petersen, Gerald W. "Punto de vista y tiempo en La Muerte de
Artemio Cruz." Revista de Estudios Hispanos 6 (enero, 1972): 85-95.

Puig, Manuel. Boquitas Pintadas. Translated by Suzanne Jill
Levine. New York: Vintage Books, 1973.

San Juan Jr., Epifanio. "Art against Imperialism." Art in Society 2:
222-225.

Sarduy, Severo. "Notas a las notas... A propósito de Manuel Puig." Revista
Iberoamericana. 37 (1971): 555-567.

Sartre, Jean-Paul. Search for a Method. New York: Vintage, 1968.

Sommers, Joseph. After the Storm. Albuquerque: University of New
Mexico Press, 1968.

Sosnowski, Saul. "Entrevista con Manuel Puig." Hispamérica 3
(1973): 69-80.

Southard, David R. "Betrayed by Manuel Puig: Reader deception and
anti-climax in his novels." Latin American Literary Review 5, No. 9 (1976):
22-28.

Tittler, Jonathan. "Order, chaos and re-order: The novels of Manuel Puig."
Kentucky Romance Quarterly 30, No.2 (1983): 187-201.

Torres-Fierro, Danubio."Conversación con Manuel Puig: La redención de
la cursilería." Eco 28 (1975): 507-515.

Vargas Llosa, Mario. La Casa Verde. Translated by Gregory Rabassa.
New York: Harper and row Publishers, 1968.

----------. Historia secreta de una novela. Barcelona: Tusquets Editor, 1971.

Villar, Luis Manuel. Carlos Fuentes: Literatura y Sociedad. Ph.D.
Dissertation, University of Wisconsin-Madison, 1982.

Weiss, Judith A. "Dynamic Correlations in Heartbreak Tango." Latin
American Literary Review 3, No. 5 (1947): 137-141.

White, Hayden. "The Fictions of Factual Language Representation."
The Literature of Fact. ed. Angus Fletcher. New York: Columbia
University Press, 1976.

Wolfgang, Luchting. "The role of Literature as a development
factor in Latin America." Research Studies 43: 132-139.

INDEX

ABOUT THE AUTHOR

Víctor Manuel Durán was born in Progreso, in the north of Belize, Central America. In 1979 he obtained his Bachelor in Education Degree from McGill University, Montreal, Canada. He then returned to his native Belize where he taught at different High Schools in the North. In 1981 he came to the United States where he received both his M.A. and Ph.D in Romance Languages, with an emphasis in Latin-American Literature from the University of Missouri-Columbia. Dr. Durán has always been interested in Marxist Literary Theory and its application to Latin-American Literature, in particular to the contemporary Spanish-American novel. Currently he is an Assistant Professor of Spanish and Spanish-American Literature at Millikin University, Decatur, Illinois.